BHARATA

The Nāṭyaśāstra

For

dearest Irene

with love and

thanks for space,

physical and intellectual

Kapila

The sculpture reproduced on the endpaper depicts a scene where three soothsayers are interpreting to King Suddhodana the dream of Queen Maya, mother of Lord Buddha. Below them is seated a scribe recording the interpretation. This is perhaps the earliest available pictorial record of the art of writing in India.

From Nagarjunakonda, 2nd century AD
Courtesy: National Museum, New Delhi

BHARATA
The Nāṭyaśāstra

KAPILA VATSYAYAN

SAHITYA AKADEMI

First published 1996

Sahitya Akademi
Rabindra Bhavan
35, Ferozeshah Road
New Delhi 110 001

Sales Section
Swati, Mandir Marg
New Delhi 110 001

Regional Offices
Jeevan Tara Building, 4th Floor
23A/44X, Diamond Harbour Road
Calcutta 700 053

172, Mumbai Marathi Grantha Sangrahalaya Marg
Dadar, Bombay 400 014

ADA Rangamandira, 109 J.C. Road
Bangalore 560 002

Madras Office
Guna Building, Nos. 304-305
Anna Salai, Teynampet
Madras 600 018

ISBN 81-7201-943-2

Rs. 150.00

Printed at : Nagri Printers, Naveen Shahdara, Delhi-110032

Contents

	Introduction	vii
1	Bharata: The Question of Authorship	1
2	The *Nāṭyasāstra:* Pre-Text and Context	13
3	The Primary Text	28
4	The *Nāṭyaśāstra:* The Implicit and the Explicit Text	47
5	The Text and Creativity	102
6	Text: The Inflow and the Outflow	113
7	The Text and the Interpreters	137
	Conclusion	162
	Bibliography	169
	Appendix: Database of *Nāṭyaśāstra*	180
	Index	**209**

Contents

Introduction

To be asked by the Sahitya Akademi to write a book on Bharata in the Biography series is a rare honour, little deserved. Had the great savants, the late Professor S.K. De, Dr Manomohan Ghosh, Dr V. Raghavan, even the late Professor K.J. Shah been alive, it would have been their prerogative. Amongst my peers and contemporaries there are Professor G.K. Krishnamoorthy, Professor G.K. Bhatt, Professor G.H. Tarlekar, Professor Kamalesh Datta Tripathi, Dr Premlata Sharma, Dr Mukund Lath and others who have spent many years of their life studying the one and only text attributed to Bharata. All of them would have been eminently suitable and far more erudite and competent.

Thus, despite the full consciousness of inadequacy, I accepted the invitation as a student of the text and its contents because it gave me the rare opportunity to ask seminal questions on the broader issues of the textual tradition in India and to re-examine this fundamental text from the point of view of vision, context, structure and process. Also, instead of a descriptive chronological account of either the author or the work, I have chosen the more hazardous path of re-investigating the methodological tools so far adopted by scholars for a critical examination of the textual tradition in general and the history of aesthetics and art criticism in particular. Consequently, the short monograph is neither a recapitulization of the histories of Sanskrit literature nor a summary of the technicalities of each of the concerns of the *Nāṭyaśāstra*, e.g. the origin of drama, the construction of the theatre, the four *abhinayas*, and the exposition of the theory of *rasa* first articulated by Bharata.

Instead, my attempt has been to re-view the *Nāṭyaśāstra* as an important confluence in the perennial flow of the tradition with the twin processes of continuity and change, as also of the interplay of the *śāstra* and the *prayoga*, not to speak of the integral vision which provides a unity of purpose and rigorousness of structure to the text.

An attempt has been made to place the text in the context of the flow of the *paramparā* rather than to locate it in a particular period and specific place. The text encapsulates a discourse in diverse disciplines and in turn stimulates further discourse in a variety of disciplines. The intrinsic multi-disciplinary nature of the text has been generally accepted but a closer examination of the system has so far not been attempted. Understandably, while some scholars have examined the chapters on aesthetics (*rasa* and *bhāva*) others have concentrated either on the chapters relating to the construction of the theatre or music or dance (including me in my previous work). Here an attempt has been made to look at the text in its totality and its well laid-out system of connections and interconnections of the parts and the whole. I hope the book will help scholars to understand the structure as also the 'systems'.

The text has a long and complex history of commentaries, interpretations, as also multiple streams of texts in the different arts which flowed out of the *Nāṭyaśāstra*. In this field also, although there has been a distinguished history of scholarship in the field of literature, particularly poetics, dramaturgy, music and dance, the dialogue between and amongst them, viewing them as emerging from a single source has been an exception rather than a rule. I have attempted to indicate the paths and tools of this dialogue in what may be called the post-Bharata period.

To encompass the history of the commentators and interpreters, the makers of aesthetic theories, in a short monograph was a daunting task. It could not be excluded because the discourse illuminates the text and reveals the nature of discourse within the tradition. A careful selection with acute discrimination of what I considered to be principal rather than secondary has been made. Naturally this has resulted in being not all 'inclusive'. The aim was to highlight the manner and nature and intellectual tools of the discourse rather than the details of the content of particular works.

Logically, this should have been extended to the interpreters of the nineteenth and twentieth centuries, i.e. critical scholarship from Regnaud to Oldenburg, Keith, Indu Shekhar, Raghavan, Masson, Christopher Byrsky and Patwardhan and others. On second thought, I decided to exclude this because no re-assessment of this history can be made without addressing issues of Orientalist discourse. This will have to be another book.

Despite its exclusion, I hope there is material here for some hitherto not so well-known information and enough stimulation to ask questions on the proverbial problems of authorship, the relationship of the oral and the written, context, text, the implicit and explicit text, and the history of discourse, not only in relation to the *Nāṭyaśāstra* but also other texts of the tradition. The relevance of these questions in the light of the contemporary debate on what constitutes a text is all too evident and needs no comment.

If further questionings arise on reading this book my task is done.

I would like to thank the Sahitya Akademi for asking me to write. I would like to acknowledge my debt to the scholars mentioned above, particularly the late Dr M.M. Ghosh, Dr Raghavan, as also Professor K.D. Tripathi for the stimulation he has provided through his lectures and many personal discussions. Dr Irene Winter, Chairperson of the Department of Art History, Harvard University, Cambridge, Mass., USA, facilitated access to the Widner Library. She and her husband, Professor Robert Hunt, not only provided space for writing much of the book but also provided the opportunity for many thought-provoking discussions on categories. These enabled me to ask unconventional questions in the context of the *Nāṭyaśāstra*. I would like to thank them. Professor B.N. Saraswati read the manuscript and his reponses were most beneficial. Professor Indra Nath Choudhury and Dr Ranjit Saha have been most gracious and understanding. I thank Shri K.D. Khanna and Shri Pawan Kalia for their invaluable assistance in typing. I am grateful to my colleague Sri Satkari Mukhopadhyaya for seeing the second page proofs.

New Delhi KAPILA VATSYAYAN
July 1995

1

BHARATA

The Question of Authorship

For the Sahitya Akademi, to choose Bharata in the 'Biography' series is as natural, almost overdue, as it is problematic and complex. The unique and undisputable importance of the *Nātyaśāstra* is universally accepted. Of the author, little is known. Thus, the very first issue one faces is that of the identity of the author, and that of the date or period of composition of the *Nātyaśāstra*.

Before proceeding to investigate who the author was, or what this historical or mythical author created, wrote or compiled, and when he did so, it would be pertinent to address the more general question of why nothing or so little is known of many Indian authors, writers, theoreticians, and of course, artists. That a culture which developed a massive macro and micro classificatory system, which had a well laid-out scheme for lineage, geneologies, schools of teaching, location and social class and caste with a remarkable penchant for categorization of pan-Indian, regional and local identities, should falter, slur over, even make secret or obliterate, the personal accounts of many authors and writers, provides a valuable clue to a deep and fundamental aspect of the culture. It points at a special approach to the work of art, its creators, as also its theoreticians. For us today the whole notion of self-identity surfaces for discussion.

Few details are known of the personal history of Vyāsa, Vālmīki, or for that matter, Kālidāsa, not to speak of the countless conceivers and builders of temples, creators of sculpture, painting, music and dance. No doubt, some among them speak about themselves, situate themselves within the lineage of their predecessors and contemporaries, and others do not. But the fact remains that personal histories are of little value, both to the authors and their critics. Coomaraswamy had spoken of the tradition of anonymity—a self-conscious transcendence from self-identity. Of late, this has been seriously questioned as scholars have found names and inscriptions on temples and sculptures, mason marks, and even signatures on paintings. Despite the discovery of these inscriptions and signatures and some details of personal lives it would be valid to ask the question, whether or not the artist/theoretician was providing inadequate information by 'volition', 'design' or 'accident' outside the work of art and none or very little of course within the work of art, other than occasionally revealing his identity.

It would appear that for the 'creator' as also the 'theoretician', the identity of 'self' as individuality, 'I-ness' as assertion of position, or point of view, that is unique, distinct, and largely in confrontation with the immediately preceding or the contemporary, was not a psychical issue. The moment of 'creation' and 'reflection', of deducing a theory or evolving a set of principles, could have been possible only after the subjective individual 'self' and 'identity' had transcended to a higher level of harmony and equilibrium, or had enlarged itself to a larger wider 'self' where principles could be evolved and universals extrapolated or explicated. Impersonalization or depersonalization was its first demand.

One can continue to discuss the perennial problems of dating and exact locations, even the historicity of many authors, writers and theoreticians. So far, a few have attributed this lack of information to the proverbial lack of a sense of history in India. Also, much time and effort has been spent in establishing chronologies, suggesting tentative dates and bringing in external and internal evidence for identifying a particular date. We believe that the near pan-India phenomenon is an indicator of a deep and fundamental world-view rather than either carelessness or casualness. Recent scholarship on Indian history has pertinently questioned the judgement of India's proverbial lack of a sense of history and time and has brought to focus the necessity of distinguishing between the notion of history and that of both *purāṇa* and *itihāsa* (so it happens). Some arguments in that context are even more relevant in the sphere of the arts.

Literary criticism and Indian art history have examined the notion of 'space' and 'time' and of place and time in relation to the work of art, poem, drama, monumental architecture, sculpture, painting, music or dance, but have not acknowledged that an alternate notion of 'space' and 'time' and that of another 'self-identity' (which, in fact, is trans-individual identity) are inter-related and intertwined. If the work of art and theoretical proposition are 'trans-self' and not individual personal-self, and if archetypes and universals are being evolved or deduced, then, while it would be important to situate oneself in a lineage of predecessors, contemporaries and even successors in the matter of 'thought', theoretical position, schools and styles, it would not be important to date oneself in mere historical time or locate oneself in a particular place, or to pay attention to dating his or her work in terms of only calendar linear time. It is true that inscriptions on temples and sculptures, colophons on manuscripts and dates on paintings provide most valuable data on time, date and place. However, at no time is all this data an indicator of the author's or theoretician's personal-self or 'I-self'. His search is not for the new unique self; instead, it is for submerging himself in a perennial flow. Invariably, he does not claim novelty or uniqueness. If and when self-consciously he identifies himself, it is only in order to situate or contextualize himself in an ongoing discourse which is larger than himself. The distinction is a fine, but important one. Also, while the information (data) on time and place except in the case of monumental architecture provides valuable material for location and date of execution, it does not follow that the date of the colophon of the manuscript or the date even on a painting or sculpture is the same as that of the composition of the work of art. In short, while details of time and place are clues for execution, they are of little avail in a critical assessment of the particular work in relation to the larger and broader river or stream of the tradition. Within this tradition, individual or group styles and schools of thought can no doubt be discerned, but again, this is not to be equated with the assertion of a unique individual-self.

A related issue is that of orality in respect of verbal texts. The text may or may not be contemporaneous with the written manuscript or text. The most outstanding case is that of the Vedic texts and their written manuscripts. Examples can be multiplied manifold in many other disciplines as also in the creative and critical arts.

It is important and necessary to make explicit these issues in the context of Indian culture in general, but especially the literary, visual and performative arts. The application of inappropriate yardsticks for comprehending a tradition has sometimes caused confusion and misconception. Undoubtedly, much time and energy has been spent on trying to 'locate', 'place' and 'date' individual authors and creators in a linear order of time and calendar and to place them in a particular 'space' and 'locale'. As a result, often, 'where' and 'when' have been the end of the investigation rather than the 'what' and 'why' of the text, work of art, or theory. Perhaps the situation can be explained through an 'analogy'. The questions asked are: by whom, when and where did the creation take place? Further, at which particular spot in the Ganga did the creation take place, if it happened in an ever-flowing river, rather than which stream flowed in or flowed out of the Ganga resulting in confluences or divergences. The human instrumentality was, no doubt, important, but in sum was an integral part of the dynamics of the nature of the flow and the course of the river. It would be more appropriate to speak of the proverbial continuity and change, and the distinctive dynamics of the Indian tradition rather than its lack of a sense of history.

These preliminary remarks will perhaps make it clear that while the exploration of the identity, date and personal history of Bharata the individual—man or woman, his/her personal life, would be an interesting course to take, it would not reveal or make manifest anything of crucial and basic importance in regard to the theory of aesthetics which was articulated or propounded in the one and only (so far acknowledged) text attributed to him, namely, the *Nāṭyaśāstra*. Our focus of attention has thus necessarily been on this seminal text, which is the first enunciation of an Indian theory of aesthetics, rather than on the person or the personal history of its author,

Bharata. Nevertheless, it would be useful to pause briefly to consider the many hypotheses which have been put forth in regard to the identity of the person Bharata.

To the question, who was Bharata and when did he live, if he did live, many answers have been suggested. There is a history of a hundred years or more of scholarship which has in part or full concentrated on the identity of Bharata the person, his possible historicity, whether or not he represented a single person or a school of thought or a group of scholars, and whether the word 'Bharata' is only an acronym or eponymous for the three syllables *Bha (bhāva), Ra (rāga), Ta (tāla)*. Some also hold the view that the *Nāṭyaśāstra* is not the work of a single author, not even of a group of authors or a school of thought. Instead, they believe that the different chapters of the book were written by different people over a period of time. Arguments and counter-arguments have been put forth for defending each of these positions. Without going into the history of these discussions by Macdonnel,[1] Keith,[2] Konow,[3] M. Ramakrishna Kavi,[4] S.K. De,[5] Manomohan Ghosh,[6] K.C. Pandey,[7] F.B.J. Kuiper[8] and many others,[9] it is necessary to point out that a close reading of the text makes it clear that the work reflects a unity of purpose and that it was the product of a single integrated vision, perhaps also of a single author. There are complexities, but no contradictions. Many subjects dealt with in the earlier chapters can only be understood by the perusal of later chapters and vice versa. Indeed, the author claims at many places that a particular sub-theme will be dealt with later, or that the chapters which come early in the sequence are in fact a condensation of details discussed later. The most obvious case is that of Chapters III and V where many technical terms of music and musical structure are mentioned. Their meaning and elaboration are contained in many later chapters where single components of sound, music, musical instruments, structure and composition are elaborated upon. The same is true of Chapter IV, known as *Tāṇḍavalakṣaṇam* which deals with the cadence of movement, called *karaṇas* and longer sequences, called *aṅgahāras*. None of the descriptions can be understood without the aid of Chapters VIII, IX and X, which deal with the macro and micro movements of the body—in short, all that Bharata recognizes as the larger rubric of *āṅgikābhinaya*. Many other instances convince one of the coherent and organically well-knit structure of the work. It could not have been the work of several authors over a long period of time. This will be obvious when the structure of the *Nāṭyaśāstra* is analysed.

Whether Bharata was a historical person or whether the author gave himself the name Bharata is a question more difficult to answer. If the work is an organic whole reflecting a single vision it would follow that the writer was a historical person who by volition made no attempt to reveal his personal identity because he believed that he represented and shared a school of thought. He was investigating a field; he was developing a theory within a larger history of discourse and laying out the broad parameters, rather than stating an individual or personal position. Logically, the mode of presentation is one of a dialogue between Bharata and sages. It is the inquiry into the nature of drama that unfolds the origin, theory and technique of drama and theatre with all its components of speech, word, body-language, gesture, costuming, décor and the inner states or temperaments. Judging from the above, it would be reasonable to assume that whoever Bharata was, he did belong to a community of artists, actors, dancers, poets, musicians, who shared a world-view—a mythology, was conversant with a textual tradition of the Vedas and was acquainted with and adept in actual performance and practice. How else would one understand a text couched in a language of mythology with repeated references to Vedic texts and rituals or *yajna*, as also to performance rites, *pūjas* ?

Nonetheless, from the text of the *Nāṭyaśāstra* we do learn something about the author as also his larger immediate artistic family of a hundred sons, if not biological descendants. The *Nāṭyaśāstra* begins by a salutation to Pitāmaha (Brahman) and Maheśvara (Śiva)—a rare combination, and attributes all that is to follow on the *śāstra* of *nāṭya* to Brahman. The sages (*muni*) approach Bharata, the master of *nāṭya* (drama), and ask him, 'How did the *Nāṭyaveda* originate? For whom is it meant?' It is in reply to this question that Bharata first insists on a state of preparedness. The listeners must be cleansed and attentive before he begins his discourse. The status of 'authority' and 'teacher' is obvious. Later, after he has told them of Brahman's state of *yoga*, his concentration and determination (*saṅkalpa*) to create a fifth Veda, the question arises of passing it on. It is here that Bharata uses the singular and says, Brahmā said to me, 'O, the sinless one, you, with your hundred sons, will have to put it (the *Nāṭyaveda*) to use.'

'Thus ordeied I learnt the *Nāṭyaveda* from Brahman and made my able sons study it as also learn its proper application' (I.24–25). Then follows a list of his hundred sons which includes names which have been identified with contemporary or later authors, specially Kohala, Dattila, Taṇḍu, Śālikarṇa. etc. This story and the listing has been the subject of some discussion in regard to identity. However, the basic information we receive from this narration is that Bharata was indeed the teacher and preceptor of a school or academy with pupils or sons, and that each of these may have been both performers and theoreticians. Bharata assigns different roles to each of the sons and thereafter the play begins.

We need not delve further into the presentation of the first play on the occasion of Indra's banner festival, but should turn our attention to the very last chapter of the *Nāṭyaśāstra* which tells us something of great significance about the group of actors (sons, pupils), if not the theoreticians.

In the last chapter of the *Nāṭyaśāstra* the author provides a definition of the appellation Bharata: 'As he alone conducts as the leader of a performance by acting in many roles and playing many instruments by providing many accessories he is called Bharata' (XXXV.91). Scholars have tried to deduce from this that the word 'Bharata' seems to denote a class of ballad singers who were perhaps precursors of drama and theatre. The *paripālavas* may well have been precursors of the actors. However, at this stage the various hypotheses need not detain us. It is only important to note here that Bharata's emphasis is on the ability of those who are called Bharatas to take on many roles and to be the vehicle of presenting and evoking *rasa* (sentiment), *sthāyi bhāva* (dominant emotive states), *vyabhicāri bhāvas* (transitory or transferable stages), etc. They are not just taking on roles; they are the instrumentalities of conveying and communicating intangible but real states of mind. The demand for impersonalization as also for discipline is inherent, as is obvious from what happens a little later in Chapter XXXV and the very last, Chapter XXXVI. These sons of Bharata obviously misuse their skills and capacities to ridicule the *muni* (sages). As a result they are cursed: 'as due to pride in your knowledge (*jñāna*) you have taken to arrogance (*avinaya*), your ill knowledge (*kujñāna*) will be destroyed.' Further, 'in the community of Sages and Brāhmaṇas you will appear as being no followers of the Vedas and will attain the character of Śūdras' (XXXVI.38).

Now, if this curse is juxtaposed with the initial exalted place given to the art as the fifth Veda, it will be clear that whether Bharata was a real person or not, the author of the text was unambiguously stating that at each moment and throughout, the actor (extended to artist) who had the power, knowledge and skill of creating another world, could at no time be arrogant, egoistic, and that he could be worthy of an exalted place, as also his art, only if he had discipline and self-restraint, self-transcendence and humility. The history of the arts and artists here or elsewhere is replete with instances of transgression of these norms and demands. Bharata, in recounting this at the end of a mighty architectonic structure of the dramatic citadel, reminds his readers that the carriers of his tradition had a responsibility precisely because the art empowered them in an extraordinary fashion.

We may be reading more into an incident which has ethical overtones, but perhaps not, because Bharata refers time and again to the power of the creative act to effect and influence and certainly evoke and stimulate reverberations of great intensity and subtlety. Appropriately, Bharata requests his sons to go through a purificatory rite (*prāyaścitta*) and requests them: 'Do not destroy this drama which has been devised with great difficulty and which depends on great things, has its origins in the Vedas, their *aṅgas* and *upāṅgas*' (XXXVI.51); and 'Know that this dramatic art has been described by Brahman himself. So teach it to your disciples and others through its practice' (XXXVI.49).

From the above, while we may not learn much about the personal history of Bharata the man, we do learn a great deal about his vision and the attitude of the author to the art. It originates through the concentration of Brahmā, is connected to the Vedas and it demands discipline and restraint from its practitioners.

The curse is not a one-time curse. Bharata is implying that whenever such transgression takes place, the artist, creator and actor would be so cursed. It is in this context that Bharata mentions that 'the rest will be related by Kohala in his supplementary treatise (*Uttaratantra*)' (XXXVI.68) and states that 'this *śāstra* has been established in heaven' and has been brought down to earth by his sons, specially Kohala, Vatsya, Śāṇḍilya and Dhurtila (Dattila). They put into 'practice this *śāstra* which augments the intellect of man, deals with the deeds of three worlds and is a specimen of all other *śāstras*'.

And finally, he once again elevates the *śāstra* when he states: 'He who hears the reading of that (*śāstra*) which is auspicious, sportful, originating from Brahman's mouth very holy, pure, good, destructive of sins and who puts into practice and he who witnesses carefully the performance will attain the same goal which masters of Vedic knowledge, performers of sacrifices or givers of gifts will attain.' (XXVI.79; M.M. Ghosh's translation.)

All these are clear enough statements about the attitude of the author, the nature of the relationship between the celestial and the terrestrial, the different orders of knowledge, the requirement of discipline and training and a final goal which must be trans-personal-self.

It is these statements which speak of an attitude of mind which is more important and basic than mere historical dating and identity of individual authorship.

We have thus to make an effort to place Bharata against the larger background and landscape of a world-view which he incorporates in his work. He shares the basic tenets of this world-view, its cosmology, its speculative thought, as also the knowledge provided by different disciplines which he utilizes profitably in creating the edifice of the theatrical universe. As one immersed in it, he is not explicit about it. We have to explicate this from the text itself rather than at this stage, the commentaries.

NOTES AND REFERENCES

1. A.A. Macdonnel, *History of Sanskrit Literature,* Munshiram Manoharlal, Delhi, 1958.
2. A.B. Keith, *Sanskrit Drama,* Oxford University Press, London, 1924.
3. Stein Konow, *Das Ind Drama,* Berlin and Leipzig, 1920.
4. M. Ramakrishna Kavi, *Introduction to the Nāṭyaśāstra,* Gaekwad Oriental series, Baroda, 1926.
5. S.K. De, *History of Sanskrit Poetics,* University of Calcutta, Calcutta, 1947.
6. M.M. Ghosh, *Introduction to the Nāṭyaśāstra,* The Asiatic Society, Calcutta, 1950.
7. K.C. Pandey, *Comparative Aesthetics,* volumes I and II, Chowkhamba Sanskrit Series Office, Varanasi, 1950, p.10.
8. F.B.J. Kuiper, *Varuṇa and Vidūṣaka on the Origin of Sanskrit Drama,* North Holland Publishing Co., Amsterdam, 1979, pp. 119 (fn. 43) and 129.
9. P.V. Kane, *History of Sanskrit Poetics,* Bombay, 1923, Introduction, pp. 8–9.

A. Hillebrandt, *Ritual Literature,* Straussburg, 1897.

2

THE NĀṬYAŚĀSTRA

Pre-Text and Context

The internal evidence of the text of the *Nāṭyaśāstra* makes it clear that the author shared a world-view, subscribed to some fundamentals and drew upon a fairly well-articulated discourse in many spheres and fields. We should examine the text itself to identify the sources of the *Nāṭyaśāstra* as also the state of knowledge and information that it reveals. This would enable us to place the *Nāṭyaśāstra* in a chronology of developments, not merely in the specific though large enough field of drama, theatre, arts, poetry, music and dance, but also in disciplines seemingly far apart such as medicine, mathematics, and of course linguistics, prosody and architecture.

A reading of the first chapter of the *Nāṭyaśāstra* and many subsequent chapters makes it clear that the author was not only acquainted with the Vedas and their status in the hierarchy of knowledge, but was familiar with the content, substance and form of each. Obviously, the authority of the Vedas was recognized at this stage. This alone could enable Bharata to cull out a theory of aesthetic and a structure of drama from the Vedas. Important is the fact that he identifies *pāṭhya,* the arti-culated spoken word, not just the word (*śabda*) from the *Ṛgveda.* The incanted word, the spoken word and its trans-mission, is a fundamental premise. So also is the case with identifying the *Yajurveda* as the source of ritual and body-language and gestures. Vedic *yajña* as a performative act is considered as a base. The methodology and structure of a total presentation must have been understood and its practice was still rigorous enough to enable the author further to compare the presentation of theatre (*nāṭya*) as being analogous to a *yajña*. The same is true in respect of the *Sāmaveda* and Bharata's identifying the musical sound, the sung note as a source. The mention of the *Atharvaveda* for drawing upon the techniques of *sāttvika* alludes to the understanding of the physio-psychical system. One could elaborate on the several allusions to Vedic practice in the *Nāṭyaśāstra* to prove that the text comes at a time when the Vedas were not a remote theoretical fountain-head, but were an immediate experience. Thus, the *Nāṭyaśāstra* is early enough in a living and vigorous tradition of both the Vedas and the Brāhmaṇas. The mention of these sources is no mere lip-service.

In another sphere, the *Nāṭyaśāstra* reveals the state and stage of development in Indian mythology We learn that the concept of Brahman, Viṣṇu, Maheśvara may have emerged, but was not yet sufficiently consolidated for the author to refer to them as the 'Trinity'. Brahman is constantly referred to as the principle of centrality and verticality in the concepts of the *brahmamaṇḍala* (on the stage), *brahmasthāna, brahmasūtra,* etc. So also is the case of Viṣṇu where he is considered as the principle of the *triangle* in *vaiṣṇavasthāna, vaiṣṇavakaraṇa,* etc. It is interesting and revealing that while Maheśa is mentioned, and there is reference to Śiva and there is the elaborate description of the *karaṇas* and *aṅgahāras,* there is no mention of Naṭarāja. The movement *bhujaṅgatrāsita,* which is the basis of the *ānanda tāṇḍava* iconography, is mentioned as only one of the *karaṇas*. Bharata is familiar with the *Ṛgvedic* myth of Purūravas and Urvaśī.

Of equal importance is the absence of Kṛṣṇa or the *rāsa* dance as a category of composition. Besides, Indra still occupies an important position, and has not been relegated to a minor deity as is obvious from a reading of Sanskrit works and evidence of Indian sculpture of the early part of the Christian era. Kārttikeya also occupies an important place and so do Umā, Pārvatī, Caṇḍikā, Siddhi and Sarasvatī. Others like Medhā, Smṛti, Mati, Niyati and Nirṛti are also visible. We know that they recede to the background fairly early.

Most significant is the absence of Gaṇeśa and the *avatāras* of Viṣṇu. Only Śiva is referred to as Ganeśvara in a couple of verses. Of great significance is the mention of the gifts Bharata receives after the successful performance. First of all, we are told 'Indra (Śakra) gave his auspicious banner (*dhvaja*), then Brahman a *kuṭilaka* and Varuṇa a golden pitcher (*bhṛṅgāra*), Sūrya an umbrella, Śiva success (*siddhi*) and Vāyu a fan, Viṣṇu a lion-seat (*siṁhāsana*), Kubera a crown and Sarasvatī—visibility and audibility' (I.60–61).[1]

This passage when compared with one occurring in the *Śatapatha Brāhmaṇa*[2] and later the *Bṛhat saṃhitā*, where similar gifts are given at the time of *yajña*, suggest that Bharata was employing a familiar mythology and cosmology in his universe of the theatre.

Scholars, particularly Kuiper, have commented elaborately on the important role of Varuṇa who holds the golden pitcher (*bhṛṅgāra*) and the significance of Brahman's giving the crooked stick *kuṭilaka* which later becomes associated with the character of the *vidūṣaka*. We are drawing attention to these verses on account of their close proximity to the Brāhmaṇas and the relative importance of Varuṇa, Vāyu and the emergence of Sarasvati already as a goddess associated with 'speech' (*vāk*) and the faculties of visibility and audibility.

Along with the mythology and the references to the *yajña* there is the important description regarding the performance of *pūjā* on the stage after the *nāṭya maṇḍapa* has been constructed. 'Perform duly in the playhouse a ceremony *yajña* with offerings, *homa, mantras*, plants (*auṣadhi*), *japa* and offerings of eatables hard as well as soft (*bhojya* and *bhaksya*)' (I.122–123). This *pūjā* is similar to the Vedic *yajña* (ritual) and according to Bharata obligatory, for he warns that 'he who will hold a dramatic spectacle (*naṭya*) without offering *pūjā* will find his knowledge and skill useless, will be reborn as animal, and will sustain a loss. Those who offer *pūjā* in accordance with all the prescribed rules of the *pūjā* (*vidhi*) will attain wealth and go to heaven' (I.125–128). It is after this that Brahmā and the other Gods said to Bharata, 'Let it be so, offer *pūjā* to the stage.' Of late,[3] this and a few other passages have received attention with a view to establish that the *Nāṭya-śāstra* drew upon *āgamic*, or by some accounts, Dravidian sources. Whether there is tension between the 'Vedic' and '*āgamic*' texts and whether they can be placed in a sequential order, is not a subject which may detain us. However, Bharata's juxtaposition of the construction of the theatre and replicating the stage as a *vedikā*, and then insistence on offerings as in a *pūjā* reveals the coexistence of two systems as also Bharata's role, once again, as a synthesizer. Obviously, he was aware of and acquainted with the elaborate procedures of rituals (*viniyoga*) of Vedic *yajna*. He carries the analogy of the *yajña* right through his text. However, he was equally aware of the necessity and efficacy of consecrating and sacralizing the space through *pūjā.* The physical space of the theatre was a micro-model of the cosmos; each deity had a demarcated place; cardinal directions were identified and the centre of the *brahmamaṇḍala* established. Through the *pūjā,* the ritual space was being consecrated (made *śubha*), 'enlivened', given presence and life. Bharata was creating an analogue at two levels. Obviously, he was familiar with the details and importance of each and he brings them together in one fold. Since the mythical world and its application as 'code' in the replication of a cosmos in ritual as also its extension into the technical literature of many disciplines is so pervasive, the mythological data provided by the *Nāṭyaśāstra* is a good clue for determining the place of the *Nāṭyaśāstra* as a comparatively early or late text. Also, quite obviously, the text comes at a time when a system of *pūjā* as distinct from the *yajña* was well established. However, there is no evidence of 'image' worship. Through the holding of a *pūjā* with *homa* and *japa,* offerings of water, food and flowers, this space would be enlivened, given breath and soul. It would acquire the same potency as an image through the ceremony of *prāṇa pratiṣṭhā.* Obviously, it was the totality of the stage which would be consecrated, rather than a particular place. In this respect the ceremonies of the *pūjā* described here become forerunners of the rituals of consecration of images described in the *āgamas.* The absence of any evidence of image worship also suggests a date prior to temple construction for the *Nāṭyaśāstra.*

The language of the *Nāṭyaśāstra* may or may not be a firm basis for determining the date of the original composition of the text in respect of its upper dating, but it is valuable for determining the lower dating. The author uses a form of Prakrit which predates Aśvaghoṣa's plays. He is aware of the close connection and yet difference between Sanskrit and Prakrit. An understanding of the use of different languages and dialects by different groups of people as also the mention of Barbaras, Kirātas and Caṇḍālas throws light on the recognition and wide acceptance of different groups of people, languages and dialects. The *Nāṭyaśāstra* provides a basis for the categorization of different groups of people. Although many of these are mentioned in the epics, both the *Rāmāyaṇa* and the *Mahābhārata*, the *Nāṭyaśāstra* gives a more systematic account of their distinctiveness.

There is also evidence of the knowledge of regional differences, as is clear from the concept of *pravṛttis*. The country is divided into cultural zones, e.g. the north, south, east and west and there is further an identification of the different modes of dress coiffure as that of Kośi, Kosala, Śaka, Pahlava and Yavana.

The ethno-linguistic data is an important source for placing the *Nāṭyaśāstra* in a chronology of the development of Indian languages, from Vedic Sanskrit to classical Sanskrit, Prakrit and the dialects. The *Nāṭyaśāstra* is written in a simple language in the *śloka* and *āryā* metres, although there are a number of prose passages. It treats its subject, like Pāṇini, as rules, even aphorisms, but each section details the aspects of the topic with a very refined analytical skill. The whole is broken up into parts and each part is examined and analysed with a view to again creating a whole.

The text reveals an amazing and staggering acquaintance with the body system, the anatomical structure, and even the physiological and psychological processes. An impressive psychosomatic system is developed. This could be possible only if the author was familiar with a flourishing system of medicine. This is evident in the chapters on the *āṅgikābhinaya* where each joint of the body is examined. The Indian understanding of the body was based on the theory of the *bhūtas* (elements) and their attributes. Anatomy placed emphasis on joints rather than muscles. A close analysis of the *Nāṭyaśāstra* reveals the author's deep understanding of the function of joints and articulation of movement. He is keenly aware of the manipulation of weight and energy.

Further, the theory of *rasa* is developed as a psycho-somatic system by establishing correspondence between the motor and sensory systems. The psychical manifests itself in the physical and the physical can evoke the psychical. The principles of tension and release are well understood. Without stating it explicitly, the author implies an adherence to the notion of the five elements (*bhūtas*) and the humours. We know that according to the Āyurvedic system of medicine equilibriums and dis-equilibriums are created by the balance or imbalance of the five elements of *agni, vāyu, pṛthvī, jala* and *ākāśa.* Indeed, the types of character enumerated in the *Nāṭyaśāstra* could emerge only from a tacit acceptance of personality types outlined in the system of Āyurveda as those of *vāta, kapha, pitta,* etc. The nature of the aesthetic experience as also the aesthetic object and character types accept the primacy of the relationship of the psychical and physical. Bharata shows a deep understanding of the senses, body and mind relationship. This is the sub-stratum of his entire work. The inner states of consciousness find expression at many levels. There is an intrinsic relationship and mutuality of mind, intellect, brain and body. Diverse configurations emerge which can be identified as distinct states of being or as what is commonly called emotive states. For Bharata, it is these states of the total human being which constitute the content of art. Also, obviously, the *Nāṭyaśāstra* follows and not anticipates the discussion on the three *guṇas* in the system of medicine. He appears to be an anticipator of the discussion on *guṇas* (qualities, attributes) in the schools of philosophy. Also, it would appear that Bharata was well acquainted with Patañjali's *yoga sūtras*, although there is no explicit statement.

Vedic mathematics, especially geometry and early trigonometry, were developed, as is evident from the making of altars in the Vedic *yajña* and the several 'measures' which were employed to construct them. Physical measure and the evolution of a system of primary units and progression in algorithms of working out ratios and proportions is fundamental to the Indian mathematical system.[4] This is as evident in ground measures as in 'sound'. Vedic incantation is a methodology of breaking sound. Again, in this sphere, the *Nāṭyaśāstra* exhibits a familiarity with the notions of space measurement, shape and form, especially in the chapters dealing with the construction of the theatre and the measurements of the three principal types of theatre (Chapter II). Further, in describing individual movements, there is an acute sense of distance, area, shape, direction, tempo and algebraic proportion. This is also evident in the matter of 'sound' intervals, micro-tone and note, as also metre in prosody. Few scholars have commented on these aspects of the *Nāṭyaśāstra*. For us, they provide a valuable clue for placing the *Nāṭyaśāstra* in a chronology of important developments in the disciplines of medicine and mathematics, especially, notions of the body and equilibriums in one case, and measure, in the other. The author tacitly accepts and applies the principles for evolving his structure of artistic creation. Indeed, the *Nāṭyaśāstra* reveals the state of the art in the physical and natural sciences as much as of speculative thought and the 'arts' *per se*.

Of equal and some fundamental importance is the fact

that the *Nāṭyaśāstra*, like many other texts—creative and critical, as also works of art—moves within the parameters of a world-view which subscribes to the goals of life as the four *puruṣārthas* and the four *āśramas*. While it identifies the goals as the four *puruṣārthas* of *dharma, artha, kāma* and *mokṣa*, and is clearly conscious of the four stages of life it makes a very radical departure from the boundaries of the *varṇa* hierarchy. His assertion that he is creating a fifth Veda which will be accessible to all castes and classes and at the same time likening it to the Vedas (i.e. creating a fifth Veda and the analogy of a ritual) transcends the accepted boundaries of hierarchy as also norms of inclusion and exclusion.

The catholic open-door attitude, obviously, came at a time when the caste structure would have been at a moment of becoming 'rigid' with rules of inclusion and exclusion. Sociologically, this breaking of boundaries and hierarchies would make the author and the text radical, if not revolutionary. The dictum that drama would include all the levels of time and place (the *trikāla* and *triloka*), the seven seas and continents, and all spheres of knowledge, the sacred scriptures, all arts and crafts, and would be open to all, comes or may have come at a time when boundaries and restrictions had become constraints and when the time was ripe to break them in certain spheres and on certain occasions. Obviously, there was categorization and differentiation. Bharata is always anxious to emphasize the synthesizing role of drama.

However, despite this radical departure at the level of social organization, Bharata shares a world-view which is reflected in the Upaniṣads and is articulated in a fairly large body of literature, including the epics. Underlying the many series of categories is the concept of *avyakta* and *vyakta* (unmanifest and manifest), of the one undifferentiated primordial state of *samādhi* and concentration and the diverse expressions. Also, it is clear that tacitly he subscribes to the *Ṛgvedic* formulation of the One formless or unformed (*arūpa*) and the multiple forms (*rūpa pratirūpa*) and the beyond form (*pararūpa*). The *Kaṭhopaniṣad* elaborates this further in the famous verse:

As the one fire has entered the world
And becomes corresponding in form to every form,
So the one Inner Soul (*antarātman*) of all things
Is corresponding in form to every form, and yet is outside.

As the one wind has entered the world
And becomes corresponding in form to every form,
So the one Inner Soul of all things
Is corresponding in form to every form, and yet is outside.

As the sun, the eye of the whole world,
Is not sullied by the external faults of the eyes,
So the one Inner Soul of all things
Is not sullied by the evil in the world, being external to it.

The Inner Soul (*antarātman*) of all things, the One Controller,
Who makes his one form manifold—
The wise who perceive Him as standing in oneself,
They, and no others, have eternal happiness!

Him who is the Constant among the inconstant, the Intelligent among intelligences,
The One among many, who grants desires—
The wise who perceive Him as standing in oneself,
They, and no others, have eternal peace!

'This is it!' —thus they recognize
The highest, indescribable happiness.
How, now, shall I understand 'this'?
Does it shine (of itself) or does it shine in reflection?

The sun shines not there, nor the moon and stars,
These lightnings shine not, much less this (earthly) fire!
After Him, as He shines, doth everything shine,
This whole world is illumined with His light.'
Know thou the soul (*ātman,* self) as riding in a chariot,
The body as the chariot.
Know thou the intellect (*buddhi*) as the chariot-driver,
And the mind (*manas*) as the reins.

The senses (*indriya*), they say, are the horses;
The objects of sense, what they range over.
The self combined with senses and mind
Wise men call 'the enjoyer' (*bhoktṛ*).

He who has not understanding (*avijñāna*),
Whose mind is not constantly held firm—
His senses are uncontrolled,
Like the vicious horses of a chariot-rider.'[5]

These assumptions which run right through the text, have to be recognized if the theory of aesthetics propounded is to be understood in its spirit and approach and not seen only as a set of rules and prescriptions at the level of skill and dexterity.

While it would be possible to give further details of the data and information revealed in the *Natyaśāstra* at the level of socio-economic structure, e.g., terms such as *sabhāstava, svāmin, yuvarāja,* even those relating to military organization (*senāpati*), along with collaborative evidence of similar terms in the inscriptions of Vasiṣṭhıputra Puḷumavi (A.C. 149) and the Junagarh rock inscription of Rudradāman (A.C. 150) prove that the writer of the *Nāṭyaśāstra* was familiar with kings and their entourage and a sophisticated urban culture; he was equally familiar with a vast variety of populace and all those we recognize as tribal and rural communities.

From the above, it would be possible to be convinced that the *Nāṭyaśāstra* is a post-Upaniṣadic text. It also precedes the composition of the earliest Purāṇas, possibly most of Sanskrit drama, and certainly the schools of philosophy. Bharata does not take the philosophic position of a particular school. This is left to his commentators and interpreters.

The text, thus, serves as an interregnum between the Vedas, Upaniṣads, early speculative thought, the disciplines of Āyurveda, early *jyotiṣa* and *gaṇita* and the later developments in mythology, as evidenced in the Purāṇas. It predates all specific works in the arts of architecture, sculpture, painting, music, dance, and of course, poetry. The mention of Buddhist and Jaina monks, the *bhikṣus, śramaṇas* and others makes it clear that the text is post-Buddha and Jain Tīrthaṅkaras (Mahāvīra). Thus, in sum, scholars are more or less agreed that the composition of the text may have taken place some time between the second century BC to second century AD, but not later.

For us, the importance of the text and its approximate dating lies in the crucial role it plays in determining the course of the flow of the river of the Indian arts, not only theatre. Once the text came into being, it gave a very definite turn to the course of the flow of tradition in many disciplines. For 1800 or 2000 years, no discussion on the arts could take place outside the parameters of the describable and indescribable word *rasa*. The categories he evolved were discussed and interpreted, but never totally rejected. The creative and critical writer accepted the fundamentals, although many changes and modifications took place. The notion of *rasa* and *bhāva* continues to be of relevance in the most contemporary styles of music and dance.

Bharata occupies a supreme place for being the master-developer of 'categories' for all the arts, particularly drama, dance, poetry, music. His distinction lies in his acumen for an uncanny precision in evolving a system of correspondence between the material, physical and the psychical, ethical and even spiritual (although the last is only implied in the text). He seeks to synthesize diverse disciplines, and asserts that the arts have the latency and potency of bringing together all aspects of life—from the physical to the psychical and even metaphysical—in a meaningful whole. The arts provide both pleasure and education and are a vehicle of beauty, duty and conduct. All this they (here, drama) achieve through the refinement of the 'senses', sense perception, particularly of the eye and the ear. Although Bharata speaks of theatre (*nāṭya*), it lays the foundation of a theory of art which is not restricted to a particular art.

The history of the Indian arts speaks of the universal applicability of the theory in all the arts. Theatre itself and the theatre-arts is an all-inclusive category with several components and sub-systems. It is obvious that at the time of writing of the *Nāṭyaśāstra* the individual arts of poetry, drama, dance and music, even architecture and sculpture and painting, were not seen as totally unrelated, insulated, autonomous genres to be observed or critically examined separately. The fact that several arts, *śilpa* and *kalā*, are mentioned, shows that there is a recognition of different types of creativity but not of insulation or absolute autonomy. The *Nāṭyaśāstra* serves as the single cohesive fountainhead for all the arts, although principally for theatre, and includes poetry, dance, music, architecture, etc.

Whether or not the *Nāṭyaśāstra* was composed or written in a particular year by a particular person is not as important a question as the fact that, like the Vedas, the *Nāṭyaśāstra* lays down the foundations of a theory and practice of the Indian arts which was adhered to by theoreticians and practising artists for a period of approximately 2000 years (until the nineteenth century or the modern period) consistently throughout the subcontinent. It had validity and applicability outside the country, especially in Asia, and continues to have relevance today for articulating a theory of art which can be clearly distinguished from Aristotelian or subsequent theories of aesthetic and art in the post-Renaissance West. The affinity between Bharata's world-view and his theory of 'imagination' and those of Longinus and Meister Eckhart and later of Blake and Yeats, is a subject too vast to be covered here. These names are being mentioned only to remind ourselves that the theory of Bharata transcends the cultural specificity of India despite its being firmly embedded in the specific culture.

NOTES AND REFERENCES

1. F.B.J. Kuiper, *Varuṇa and Vidūṣaka on the Origin of Sanskrit Drama*, North Holland Publishing Co., Amsterdam, 1979, p. 144 for the significance of the gifts; also Kapila Vatsyayan, *The Square and the Circle of the Indian Arts*, Roli Books International, New Delhi, 1983, p. 43.
2. Stella Kramrisch, *The Hindu Temple*, University of Calcutta, Calcutta, 1946, pp. 246–47; Kapila Vatsyayan, *The Square and the Circle of the Indian Arts*, pp. 45–47; Julius Eggeling, *Śatapatha Brāhmaṇa*, Sacred

Books of the East series, 4 vols., Oxford University Press, London, 1866, Vol. XXVI.

3. Natalia Lidova, *Drama and Ritual of Early Hinduism,* Motilal Banarsidass, Delhi, 1994; Saraswati Amma, *Geometry in Ancient and Medieval India,* 1979, pp. 30 and 40.
4. Kapila Vatsyayan, *The Square and the Circle of the Indian Arts,* pp. 77–78.
5. *Kaṭhopaniṣad,* translated by Robert Ernest Hume, Third Valli, Verses 3–5.

3

The Primary Text

Although the internal evidence of the *Nāṭyaśāstra* enables us to contextualize the text within the larger matrix of the Indian cultural tradition at the level of concept, speculative thought, mythology, ritual traditions, both Vedic and others, when it comes to the written manuscripts of the text, there have been and continue to be complex, unresolved problems if not unsurmountable hurdles.

As has been pointed out before, there is a broad consensus amongst scholars that the date of composition of the *Nāṭyaśāstra* is somewhere between second century BC to second century AD.[1] The written manuscripts so far located belong roughly to the period between the twelfth and the eighteenth centuries. During the intervening period, either manuscripts were lost, or alternately the text was not transcribed to writing. No written evidence is available for nearly one thousand years or more after its composition. A further complication arises on account of the fact that although the date of the greatest commentator Abhinavagupta is known (tenth to eleventh century AD), manuscripts of the *Abhinavabhāratī* are also not contemporaneous with the writing of the *Abhinavabhāratī*.

While the *Nāṭyaśāstra* may have been transmitted orally on account of its cryptic aphoristic verses, the text of the *Abhinavabhāratī* is monumental, largely in prose. How was this transmitted, or is it a case of destruction of all manuscripts of an earlier period, specially in northern India —the home of the author of the *Abhinavabhāratī,* if not Bharata?

These are knotty problems which remain unresolved. The history of scholarship on the *Natyaśāstra* is based on the incomplete and complete manuscripts of both the *Nāṭyaśāstra* and the *Abhinavabhāratı.* The manuscripts have been sometimes so corrupt that one scholar remarked that 'even if Abhinavagupta descended from heaven and had seen the manuscript he would not easily restore its original meaning. It is in fact an impenetrable jungle through which a rough path now has been traced.'[2]

It will be clear from the above that as in the case of identity and date of the author, the establishment of an authentic text has been a complex matter. Each time two sets of problems have to be resolved. This is true not only of the *Nāṭyasastra* but is relevant to a large corpus of knowledge in the Indian tradition.

First is the question of orality—an aspect we have referred to earlier. The composition itself is the word-heard rather than the word-written. The word-heard—articulated, intonated—is perennial and immutable, as in the case of the Vedas (*sruti*); the safeguard of its precise exactitude and purity is a matter of a great and grand system of oral transmission. The Vedic corpus could be preserved for centuries only because of the system of intonation and recitation which broke down the word not only to its syllabic value but more. It was and is preserved through a variety of recitative systems we recognize as the *śākhās.*

What is exact and precise in respect of the *śrutis* (Vedic corpus) may not have been so in the case of the narrative or epic because 'memorization' was in a single system and not in a variety of permutations and combinations of the syllables or phonemes. Nevertheless, the recitative epic tradition gave a distinctive flavour to the creative word. The written text, whenever it was transcribed, was considered authentic or otherwise on the basis of language, grammar, metre and style. Many faulty manuscripts were and have been restored on this basis.

In the case of critical and technical writing in verse or prose, the text was largely aphoristic in quality—a number of pithy, concise statements—with little argument or discursiveness. Such compositions were and are also capable of being easily memorized and transmitted. There was and is a binding unity of subject, 'theme' and the transmission can be and has been often exact without the aid of the complex system of Vedic intonation. The composition of these texts invariably reflects a quintessence of a larger deeper discourse, never made explicit in language. The 'words' and *sutras* or aphorisms, serve as memory aids, so to say, for both the teacher and the pupil. The teacher transmits the text orally to the pupil even if he is working with a written text precisely because the text itself is only a springboard for communicating all levels of meaning of the text and placing it in the larger background and context of the discourse in the particular discipline. This is *paramparā*—the process of transmission.

While the question, what is the nature of the text and the oral composition and transmission, is primary, the second set of problems arise when this body of creative and critical writing is transcribed and now becomes a written text. The date of the composition of the text and the dates of the first written manuscripts of the text are hardly ever contemporaneous until the tenth or precisely fourteenth or sixteenth centuries. In some cases the hiatus between the oral and the written in terms of time and duration continues well into the eighteenth century.

Sometimes, in evaluation and critical assessment, these obvious and self-evident facts are ignored, or at least overlooked. The implications of critically evaluating a work on the basis of a late correct or corrupt transcription as the written text has led to critical judgements which may or may not have anything to do with the original text. So, what or which is the authentic text ?

Much of Sanskrit literature and knowledge in highly specialized fields is known to us through written manuscripts of varying dates (largely, post fourteenth or fifteenth centuries AD, only a very few of the twelfth century AD) although the original compositions may go back to second century BC or second century AD or fourth century AD or slightly later. A composition must have been fairly pervasively known in different parts of India for it to be transcribed to writing in different parts of India. Many manuscripts reveal a pan-Indian spread where manuscripts of the same work are found in different parts of India. Amongst these, the earliest are the Gilgit manuscripts, followed by those preserved in Nepal or Tibet.

Before taking up the question of the text of the *Nāṭyaśāstra*, and what it contains, this general remark about the nature of its textuality in general terms is necessary. 'Unlike a modern piece of writing or even some Greek or medieval Indian or European writing, at no time are we looking at an absolutely authentic text, written or typed by the author himself!'

The manuscript reflects a transcription or a minimal reduction of an oral text, faithful or otherwise. Its many manuscripts are all transcriptions, which in the language of traditional scholarship we call recensions.

The history of the discovery of the manuscripts and the attention given to the *Nāṭyaśāstra* throws interesting light on recent scholarship, its limitations, as also the opportunity the primary material presents for hypothesizing and for multiple readings. While more could be said on the nature of the critical discourse on the *Naṭyasastra* in the nineteenth and twentieth centuries, some details of the discovery of the manuscripts of the *Nàṭyaśāstra* may not be out of place here, especially because the views held by these distinguished pioneers held sway for a century or more.

As is well-known, William Jones' attention was drawn to the manuscript of *Śakuntalā* in 1784 and published a translation in 1789. At this time there was no mention of the existence of a theoretical base of the structure of the drama. While the publication was hailed far and wide and Goethe showered praise on its poetry and lyricism, he bemoaned the Sanskrit dramatist's lack of a sense of organic structure: 'A great tree in a fragile delicate vase.' Perhaps he may have changed his views had he been acquainted with even a corrupt text of the *Nāṭyaśāstra.* Wilson wrote extensively on Sanskrit literature and drama and we are all indebted to him for his translations. He presented us with select specimens of the *Theatre of the Hindus* in 1826. In the introduction he deeply lamented the loss of the manuscripts of the *Nāṭyaśāstra.* Hall did lay his hand on a single manuscript, could not complete editing it and did not make use of it in editing the *Daśarūpaka* published in the *Bibliothica Indica* series (Calcutta, 1861–65). He did, however, print the relevant chapters of the *Nāṭyaśāstra* as appendices. Haymann, a German scholar, wrote the first article on the *Nāṭyaśāstra* in 1874 on the basis of a manuscript. He described the contents.[3] P. Regnaud, a French scholar, found another manuscript and published parts of Chapters XV and XVI and Chapter XVII (i.e. those dealing with prosody, metrical patterns and diction) in the *Annales de Musée Guimet,* II

Tome in 1884, and followed this with the publication of Chapters VI and VII in the same year under the title of *Rhetoric Sanscrite.* A pupil of Regnaud, J. Grosset continued the interest of his teacher and published in 1888 Chapter XXVIII (on music) under the title *Contribution a l'étude de la musique Hindoo* (Lyons, 1888). Sylvan Levi, who wrote the important book *Theatre Indien* in 1890, apparently did have access to two or three manuscripts He chose not to examine them closely for critically assessing the nature of Indian theatre. Since he was primarily concerned with the literary form of the plays, his attention was drawn to the chapters dealing with the use of language (Chapter XVIII of the M.M. Ghosh edition) and the discussion on styles (*vṛttis*) (Chapter XXII). He displays some acquaintance with the contents of the chapter on diction and on the classification of the types of plays (Chapter XX). It is interesting to note, that Levi did not consider it necessary to look at the text as a whole or establish any meaningful relationship between the text and the Sanskrit drama. Nevertheless, he made an invaluable contribution by focussing attention on the existence of such a text.

J. Grosset, on the other hand, persevered with his initial interest, examined all the manuscripts he could lay his hands on, and published in 1898 the text comprising Chapters I to XIV under the title *Treate du Bharata sur la Theatre Text Sanscrit edition critique* Tome I Partie I *(Annales de la Universitie de Lyons,* Fas. 40, 1898)

Independent of the interest in France and Germany, Russia (Oldenberg), etc. Pandit Shivadatta and Kashinath Pandurang Parab identified two other manuscripts and on this basis published in 1894 an edition which we know as the familiar *Kāvyamālā* edition.

Enough interest had been created by these publications, partial or complete, to hunt for more manuscripts.

Ironically, alongside the critical evaluation on Indian theatre continued, largely on the basis of Wilson's and Lévi's writings, both largely unacquainted with the *Nāṭya-śāstra.*

Between 1900 and 1926, as a result of the hunt for more manuscripts and the momentous discovery of the manuscript of the *Abhinavabhāratī* in Kerala, the first critical edition of the *Nāṭyaśāstra* was edited by M. Rama-krishna Kavi and published in the *Gaekwad Oriental series* in 1926. In the preface to this edition, he provides some details of the manuscripts of the *Nāṭyaśāstra* he located in different parts of India and in the libraries of Nepal. While he does not give full details, he speaks of forty manuscripts and two recensions—one northern and the other southern—and a shorter and a longer version. Despite the difficulty of dealing with the text of the *Abhinavabharatī*, a valiant effort was made and it is this published edition with all its shortcomings that has been the basis of all subse-quent scholarship. Other than a small handful of scholars who have looked at the original primary material, Kavi certainly did make a pathway for exploring what he called 'the jungle of *Abhinavabhāratī*' and provided the basis of a critical dialogue for six decades or more, from 1926 to date. A second edition of the first volume appeared in the *Gaekwad Oriental series*, after a lapse of thirty years in 1956. The editór, K.S. Ramaswami Sastri, made a heroic effort to fill the lacunae, correct readings and consult more or at least the same manuscripts which Ramakrishna Kavi had consulted. Both Kavi and Ramaswami also tried to relate the verbal text of Chapter IV, *Tāṇḍavalakṣaṇam*, with the sculptural reliefs of the *karaṇas* in the *gopurams* of the Chidambaram temple. It may be pointed out that with the publication of the 1926 edition and its revision in 1956 the interest in the *Nāṭyaśāstra* had shifted, or certainly extended, from the purely literary and poetic aspects to identifying sculpture on the basis of this text, on the one hand, and the interpretation of the text on the basis of philosophic schools, on the other. The text of the *Abhinavabhāratī*, in whatever corrupt or difficult form, was a clear and unambiguous invitation for the study of Kashmiri Śaivism, as also exploration of the diverse philosophic schools mentioned in the *Abhinavabhāratī*. The publication of the *Abhinavabhāratī*, opened up a whole new debate on the number of *rasas*, whether eight or nine. Is *śānta* one more *rasa* or is it inherent in the eight? This resulted in an impressive corpus of critical literature. For a time it appeared that Abhinavagupta had overshadowed or replaced Bharata and the *Nāṭyaśāstra*. We shall evaluate Abhinavagupta's contribution later, but at this stage, the history of the discovery and publication of the text on the basis of manuscripts is being outlined only to underline the fact that there are some inherent difficulties in determining an *authentic* text or an objective text. It is the desire for establishing an authentic text that leads to continued editions.

In the case of the *Nāṭyaśāstra* another edition was published from Banaras in 1929 in the *Kashi Sanskrit series*, to be followed by the most popularly used edition and translation by Manomohan Ghosh brought out by the Asiatic Society in 1950 and 1956. A recent attempt has been made by a group of scholars (unidentified) and another edition has appeared in 1993. In-between, there were editions in the Marathi, Gujarati and Tamil scripts, and translations in Indian languages.

The search for manuscripts, as also for establishing an authentic text of the *Nāṭyaśāstra*, continues. Over these forty years, many efforts have been made, the most recent being of the establishment of a project in Ujjain for another critically edited text of the *Nāṭyaśāstra.* It is understood that nearly fifty-two manuscripts of the text have been identified and transcripts have been made. The very nature of the text called for a team of scholars with specialization in different disciplines to tackle the different chapters. The last is a significant insight into the integral vision of a Bharata or an Abhinava and the fragmented but highly specialized skills of modern scholarship. Be that as it may, the tentative findings of this group, especially K.D. Tripathy who is directing the effort, is that the theory of M. Ramakrishna Kavi of a northern and a southern recension, as also a shorter or longer version, has to be seriously questioned if not totally abandoned. Indeed, the editor of the second edition of the *Gaekwad Oriental series,* Ramaswami, also holds the same view. It is necessary to highlight this fact because the division of many manuscripts into southern and northern recensions has been in many cases a superimposition of a tacit acceptance of marked differences in northern and southern recensions. In this case, the fact of the matter is that Abhinavagupta was a northerner but the closest approximation to his text is a manuscript in the Trivandrum collection. Other instances can be given. The more pertinent question to be asked is as to the manner and mode of transmission of a single text to different parts of India—ranging from Nepal, Almora to Ujjain, Darbhanga, Maharashtra, Bengal, Andhra, Tamilnadu and Kerala. All these manuscripts can be dated roughly between the twelfth and the eighteenth centuries, with the exception of those of the commentator—Udbhaṭa. One of his works was found in the Gilgit manuscripts (tenth to eleventh century), now edited by Gnoli. The earliest manuscripts come from Nepal in Newari script. The text is available in many scripts—Newari, Devanagari. Grantha, Tamil, Telugu and Malayalam.[4]

Whatever the difficulties of arriving at an authentic text from the point of view of scholastic research, the sheer extensiveness of the primary material of a technical text speaks of a living vibrant tradition where the practice (praxis) and performance and its critical discourse were complementary and mutually supportive. The reasons for Kerala being the strongest inheritor of the Sanskrit drama in performance in a form like *Kūṭiyāṭṭam* may perhaps be attributed as much to the genius of a Kulaśekhara as to the seminal effect of the *Nāṭyaśāstra* and *Abhinavabhāratī.*

To return, however, to the search for location of more manuscripts and the present stage of scholarship, the last systematic effort is that of the Indira Gandhi National Centre for the Arts, which has created a computerised database of the manuscripts so far locatable in public and private libraries. It is attempting to microfilm and electronically store the several versions of the text to facilitate further search, research and scholarship. Details of the manuscripts so far entered are given in Appendix I. This is by no means exhaustive.

Some detailed account of the history of the discovery, editing and publication of the text, was necessary to underscore the fact that many critical evaluations and judgements have been made on the basis of a particular reading in a specific manuscript or edition.

However, even more important is the fact that the written text (i.e. manuscript) is an indicator of or the closest approximation to the original (oral or written). The author (original) may or may not have taken a very 'rigid' individualistic position in regard to his text. We have pointed out earlier that eschewment of his personal 'I-ness', the individual position, was a primary demand. His text, in the first place, was transpersonal and represented a larger flow, and perhaps the original author may have insisted on an authenticity of spirit, attitudes and parameters rather than semantics and words. His text or written text may well have been only a memory-aid or a 'code' in a community of scholars who were familiar with the larger and deeper communication through the oral word and practice. These are questions for Sanskrit scholars to confront. So far scholarship at one level, and rightly so, has been concerned with establishing an authentic text (leaving aside the questions of grammar, etymologies, scribes, errors, etc.). In the case of the *Nāṭyaśāstra* at least it is conceivable that the author was perhaps stating as precisely as possible, almost as a condensation, rules and regulations of creation, performance and reception in a larger tradition of theoretical discourse, performance, practice and of oral transmission. The text itself, then, in its very structure, makes room for fluidity of interpretation and allows for multiple ways of understanding it. Truly, Bharata's initial statement that 'I am creating a theory and text of performance, of practice and experimentation' acquires crucial importance. The composer of the text consciously creates a fluid text. He calls it a *sastra* of *prayoga*, i.e. a theory of praxis. This seeming paradox is, in fact, a foundational principle on which his edifice is created. This is evident from several statements by Bharata, where after a number of rules and regulations have been stated with utmost calm, he states that 'these can be changed according to the needs of time and place'. The manuscript and a discussion on the nature of the text, has brought us to assess the textual tradition in India, as almost an anticipator of the latest contemporary discourse on whether a text has an objective status, can it be absolute or authentic at any time. Its authenticity and value lies in its capacity for variant and multiple readings. Bharata appears to be conscious of the fact that there would be the probability of his text being read, interpreted and performed in a number of ways, even from diverse points of view.

It is interesting that the text of the *Nāṭyaśāstra* and the statements made by its author sound familiar as distantly related to the post-modern discussion on a text. In the case of the *Nāṭyaśāstra,* not only has the text been variously interpreted by different readers and disciplines, but the author himself allows for varied interpretations and readings, even modifications of his own injunctions. Indeed, in the Indian tradition, certain types of oral texts are fixed, frozen and unchanging (e.g. *śruti* and some others) and the written texts (*smṛtis*) are fluid and changing. The *Nāṭyaśāstra* is an excellent example of this phenomenon. Flexibility is in-built in the very structure of a text.

In order to understand the text in the Indian tradition an analogy would be pertinent. Whether it is the *Mahābhārata* or the *Nāṭyaśāstra,* these are texts with a seed which has a distinctiveness, like a genetic distinctiveness. It grows like a tree and it gives out shoots like *aśvatha.* In the case of the *Nāṭyaśāstra* the possibility of multiple readings is in-built in the text; it does not explicitly state the possibilities of multiple texts or multiple writing. However, as we shall observe in a later chapter, it is from the seeds of this very text that other trees grow.

Before we examine more closely the structure and contents of the *Nāṭyaśāstra,* it may also be useful to pause here to consider not only the general nature of a text—verbal, oral or written—but the pointed question of what constitutes a *śāstra* in the Indian tradition generally, more specifically in the arts. Why is a category of writing called a *śāstra?*

There have been countless equivalents of the word

śāstra in English, of 'theory', 'code', 'manual', 'treatise', 'scientific text'. Also, *śāstra* is distinguished in literature and the arts as being a category distinct from the creative. While in the English language, we can easily use the terms 'creative and critical literature', 'creative and technical literature', when the terms are transferred to the sphere of the Indian, for that matter, the Asian arts, there is some difficulty. Can we juxtapose *kāvya* (poetry, epic or lyrical) and *śāstra*, and *nāṭya* (drama) and *śāstra* as being opposites or use a generic term as *kalpanā* (imagination) and *racanā* (composition) or and use the word *śāstra* as an antonym or perhaps coin a pair *sāhitya* (literature) and *samālocanā* (criticism) or *kavitā* (poetry) and *samālocanā* (criticism) as in contemporary parlance in Hindi and other literatures?

The *śāstra* within the tradition cannot be equated, so far as one can gather, from the *śāstras* in different fields and disciplines, to 'critical writing' or criticism, as used in contemporary scholarship.

Can we then equate the category of *śāstra* with theory, and then use it for the spheres of *dharma, nīti, cikitsā*, etc.? Can we juxtapose the term with the antonym of 'practice' and suggest another pair of binary opposites of modern discourse, i.e. of 'theory' and 'praxis'? Or, can we speak of *śāstra* only as prescriptive and understand the word *prayoga* as experimentation and innovation as used in contemporary Indian literatures, specially, Hindi?

Let us look at both these levels. First, the domains of human activity and knowledge covered by the texts which can be categorized as *śāstra* and second, the adjectival and adverbial use of the term when used as *śāstrīya nṛtya, śāstric*, etc.

In regard to the first, one knows that within the Indian tradition, the range of subjects covered by the *śāstras* is extensive, as they cover all possible human activities—from cooking to horse and elephant breeding, performing, love-making to social conduct, economic organization, justice and much else and, of course, all the arts—from architecture to poetry. Now, if we look at this range closely, we will find that all these activities and disciplines are subsumed in the three more basic categories of human endeavour defined in the Indian world-view. Amongst the four-fold spheres and goals (i.e. *puruṣārthas*), the *śāstras* relate to the sphere of *dharma, artha* and *kāma,* but not *mokṣa* the final. There is, for example, no *ātman* or *mokṣa śāstra* although the goal of each of these may be *mokṣa* (liberation) The exclusion of the last is a pointer to a recognition of a dimension of life endeavour where classifications, 'grammar' rules, or even intellection is of little significance. One could deduce from this that *śāstras* are in the sphere of measure, of 'organization', of 'methodologies' alluding to the infinite perhaps, but are in the finite. In common parlance, the Purāṇas and other texts are alluded to as *mokṣa śāstra,* but these should only be considered as the texts that lead to *mokṣa,* but are not texts of *mokṣa.*

Now, if we look at some of these texts, specially in the arts, we find that they are largely couched in a cryptic language which often sounds like algebraic formulae and is, at least on the surface, prescriptive. Little wonder that they have been called 'recipe' books for cooking meals. In common parlance, they have been described through several English equivalents such as 'treatise', 'manual', 'codes', etc.[5]

In regard to the second level, i.e. juxtaposing the terms 'theory' and 'praxis' with *śāstra* and *prayoga,* or using the adjectival forms of *śāstrīya saṅgīta, nṛtya,* etc., we find that the *Nāṭyaśāstra* at least does not consider *śāstra* and *prayoga* (i.e. theory and praxis) as antonyms or in opposition. Instead, Bharata asserts at the very outset that he is writing a *prayoga śāstra.* Translated literally in modern usage, it would amount to saying that he is writing a 'theory' of 'praxis'. We may even suggest that he is alluding to a prescriptive text of 'praxis' and 'practice'. Paradoxical as it may sound, this is indeed what he sets out to do, and what distinguishes his work as also of others, both from being cook-books or manuals on the one hand, and abstract theoretical discourses, on the other. The dictionary meaning of the word *śāstra* (Monier-Williams) as an order, a command, rule, teaching, direction, instruction manual, conforming to sacred precepts, would obviously need considerable modification and explanation if we are to evaluate these categories from within the tradition on its own terms, before equating them with others which carry with them a valid and legitimate 'load' of another stream of thought and discourse. The English word 'theory', with its long, distinguished and perfecuy understandable history, implies knowledge or pure science as such without reference to applicability. Further, it is accepted that a theory is a tentative statement of a supposed principle or relationship of cause and effect, in short, a working hypothesis. In its derivative and extended meaning, it suggests abstract principles and universals of any body of related facts.

The category of '*śāstra*' does not denote the purely speculative and contemplative—it may or does suggest abstraction of principles from a body of facts, or more precisely, the phenomenon of practice. It is in this sense and with these improvisos that we have used the word 'theory' for *śāstra* in this discussion.

The *Nāṭyaśāstra* as a text has to be viewed, thus, neither as 'theory' as understood in its Greek connotation, nor as a 'manual' or a series of 'commands' or precepts of sacred knowledge. It is a 'category' apart, which moves on many levels, some implicit, others explicit and explanatory. It is, as it were, an abstraction, a deduction from experience and practice, and in turn can play an inductive role. The sifting of a large body of data in a particular field of activity of human life and its systemized arrangement as broad principles are its distinguishing features. The fundamentals so proposed are subject to both multiple interpretations and modifications in a specific time, place and situation.

As regards the recent use of the term *śāstra* as adjective, *śāstrīya nṛtya* or *saṅgīta,* it suggests quality of performance, sometimes genre, with an implied translation of the term 'classical' in English, as a qualitative and not historical period category.

Elsewhere,[6] we have elaborated on the jigsaw puzzle of categories and terms in Sanskrit and their English equivalents. Here, it is necessary to draw attention to the particular category of knowledge and discourse to which our text belongs within a larger body of knowledge and its epistemology.

As has been pointed out, Bharata is at pains to remind his readers and listeners repeatedly that the efficacy of the formulation lies in practice (*prayoga*); also, that the text can be interpreted and changed according to the needs of 'time' and 'place'. He allows for both continuity and flow, as also change.

We have also to take into account the 'dynamics' of the oral and the 'written', more, the silent shared experience and transmission in words. The algebraic formulae or aphoristic character was natural and understandable because like modern software with codes, the articulated word was only an indicator, stimulator of a larger shared and transmitted knowledge. Initiated training and practical experience was essential.

The *nātya* or *vāstu* or *śilpa śāstras* existed within a cultural milieu of (a large body of) shared and transmitted knowledge, practical expertise, and systemized methodologies of oral transmission. The written texts, as they have come down to us through manuscripts and published editions, represent a 'residual' record of this larger and also more exact communication. They are not the totality; they only reflect a 'totality' and have to be viewed as such.

The history of the search and discovery of the manuscripts, the fragmentary nature of the evidence, the endeavour of arriving at one authentic text, has now to be juxtaposed with the need to recognize the larger cultural matrix, the categories of knowledge and discourses evolved and the methods of transmission.

The text is the one and only evidence we have—indispensable and invaluable—and yet each text is perhaps a fragment or a small prototype of a great monument, not of 'bricks' and 'stones', but of experience, speculation, thought and practice, shared and lived.

One last point in the context of the textual tradition of the Indian arts is pertinent. Can any text in the Indian arts be considered exclusive in terms of the modern categories of architecture, sculpture, painting, music, dance, drama and poetry? Are the categories of *vāstu, śilpa, citra, saṅgīta, nāṭya, sāhitya, kāvya* insulated, autonomous, inclusive or exclusive? If not, then, what is the internal interdisciplinary or interpenetrating system? How do these texts, and the *Nāṭyaśāstra* as the earliest of them all, approach the question of the autonomy and specificity of each art-form and its intrinsically inter-related character?

An examination of these texts, except in the case of

poetics and rhetorics, reveals that in each case the particular *śāstra* (*nāṭya* or *vāstu* or *saṅgīta*) identifies a principal genre or form and then invariably considers the role of the other arts in the structure of the principal. Thus, drama (*nāṭya*) not only considers but comprises architecture, dance, music, poetry and painting. *Vāstu* (architecture) comprises sculpture, painting and dance, and *saṅgīta* (music) considers the physiological systems, poetry and dance and so on. There is an integral vision which blooms in a multiplicity. It is not an aggregation of disciplines. It is an interpenetration of disciplines. For facility, we may call it an integral multidisciplinary approach.

We shall endeavour to look at the *Nāṭyaśāstra* at its implicit and explicit levels, its structure and design, the inter-relatedness of the arts and its language of form and technique, throughout reminding ourselves that our text is neither pure theory nor a working hypothesis or manual or rule-book or a handy guide for practitioners of the arts. Instead, it reflects a world-view, is embedded in a cultural context, shares a vast body of knowledge in many disciplines, was perhaps orally transmitted for centuries through a highly systemized methodology of transmission, teacher to pupil, pedagogic schools, is inter- and multidisciplinary in nature, and is pan-Indian.

The *Nāṭyaśāstra* is an ocean, certainly a confluence. An attempt at analysis can only be inadequate despite the fact that from the sixth century to the eighteenth century it was followed and commented upon, and now for a hundred years or more, modern scholarship has attempted a critical assessment of the seminal text.

NOTES AND REFERENCES

1. Manomohan Ghosh, Introduction to the *Nāṭyaśāstra,* Royal Asiatic Society, Bengal, 1950, p. xxvi; all references and translations are of this edition unless otherwise indicated. M. Ramakrishna Kavi, *Nāṭyaśāstra,* Gaekwad Oriental series, Baroda, second edition 1956, Preface to first and second editions; P.V. Kane, Introduction to *History of Sanskrit Poetics,* 1923, pp. viii–ix, where he discusses dates.
2. M. Ramakrishna Kavi, Preface to the first edition of the *Nāṭyaśāstra,* Vol. I, Oriental Institute, Baroda, 1926, p. 63.
3. Haymann, 'Ueber Bharata's *Nāṭyaśāstram*' in *Nachrichten von der Koeniglichen, Gesellschaft der Wissenschaften Goetingen,* 1874, p. 86.
4. K.S. Ramaswami Sastri (ed.), *Nāṭyaśāstra,* Baroda edition, 1956; for details of manuscripts, recensions, scripts and chronology see Preface to first and second editions, GOS, 1926 and 1956. Also see M.M. Ghosh, *Nāṭyaśāstra* (translation), Introduction, 1950; F.B.J. Kuiper, *Varuṇa and Vidūṣaka on the Origin of the Sanskrit Drama,* 1979.
5. A. Dallapicolla, *Śāstric Traditions in Indian Arts,* Vols. I and II, Steiner Verlag, Wiesbaden, 1989, Introduction, and following articles: Kapila Vatsyayan, 'Inaugural Address'; T.S. Maxwell, 'Śilpa versus Śāstra', pp. 3–16; Sheldon Pollock, 'Idea of Śāstra in Traditional India', pp. 17–27. Also D.H.H. Ingalls, *Dhvanyāloka,* Harvard University Press, Cambridge, MA, 1990, 'Introduction', where he uses the term 'Scientific Treatise'.
6. Kapila Vatsyayan, *Ludwik Sternbach Memorial Lecture,* Vol. I, Akhil Bhāratīya Sanskrit Pariṣad, Lucknow, 1979, pp. 783–804.

4

THE NĀTYAŚĀSTRA

The Implicit and the Explicit Text

In an earlier chapter, we have drawn attention to the cultural context of the *Nātyaśāstra*, and the developments which had taken place in several spheres of Indian life and thought. In the preceding chapter, the present-day limitations of viewing a verbal, written text, which in its very nature is a residual quintessential record of a deeper, richer experience and wider discourse, and not an absolute autonomous product, were pointed out. The *Nātyaśāstra*, like other texts in several disciplines, has implicit and explicit layers. Some insight can be gained by penetrating through the language of 'myth', 'legend' and the anecdotes in which it is couched. There is, as it were, a 'code' of discourse which is expected to be evident and illuminating to the initiated and trained. On the surface, it is engaging and interesting to the general or 'lay'

A very careful sifting of these layers is thus necessary: both of the unsaid, unspoken but equally unambiguous levels, and the more evident explicit levels of structure, methodology and technique.

At the very outset, Bharata's text makes it clear that he shares the world-view of his predecessors, its cosmology and mythology. The inspiration of the creation is acausal and transmundane, born from reflection and meditation (*saṅkalpa* and *anusmaraṇa*). At the level of articulation, the endeavour (enterprise, in modern discourse) is comprehensive. Here, all branches of knowledge (*vidyā*), the sciences and the arts, all dimensions and orders of 'space' and 'time' are encompassed. Its scope is all-embracing. It deals with the universe (*sarvaloka*). Implicitly, it suggests an *ādhidaivika* level (super-mundane, not to be confused with 'sacred') of experience at the initial stage (I.13–16).

Stated differently, Bharata not only acknowledges debt and identifies the sources of his work, but also outlines the broad parameters of his work and the parallel levels at which his text will proceed. It is not necessary for him to state explicitly that the three levels—*ādhidaivika* (divine), *ādhyātmika* (both spirit and self) and *ādhibhautika* (material) constitute the tacit framework, so also the *puruṣārthas*. So, from a 'divine', an acausal origin of a happening in no time, a revelation, an intuitive experience, drama is born. It has a structure and form. Its tools are the two primary sense perceptions of sound and speech. It deals with the visible and audible, employs body language (gestures), speech, music, dress, costume and an understanding of psychic states, which involuntarily reflect themselves in the physical body, e.g., tears, horripilation, etc., to express and convey meaning and emotive states.

But, behind it all is the assimilation and acceptance of a world-view, a true familiarity with the discourse on life phenomena and a body of speculative thought with its refined and chiselled key concepts. Some amongst these already assume the status of technical terms; others are frequent in discussion. Alongside, as we have pointed out earlier, is both the familiarity with the structure and the detailed methodology of the *yajña*. Bharata draws from both in conceiving and visualizing his theatrical universe.

Elsewhere, a fuller elaboration has been attempted of the world-view, the speculative thought, methodology and system of the Vedic ritual (*yajña*) which is relevant for comprehending both the intent and the structure of the theatrical universe enunciated by Bharata.[1] Without repeating the full argument, it would be useful to recapitulate the essentials of this world-view and emergent cosmology, as this is the implicit dimension of the text which provides a unity and cohesiveness to the explicit manifested variegated level of the *Nāṭyaśāstra.* Only a few key principles of the world-view and the metaphors used to comprehend the phenomena need be mentioned.

First and foremost, the world is an organism, a whole with each part inter-related and interdependent. This is basic and fundamental. The key word and metaphor of this comprehension is *bīja* (seed). The process of growth, the proliferation of each part being distinct and different, and yet developing from the same unitary source, is fundamental. While on earth, the physical reality of 'seed' (*bīja*) is seminal, in the sky '*sūrya*' (sun), *agni* (fire) is the activizing principle of the universe. Logically, the connection between the 'seed' (*bīja*) on earth as matter and fire '*sūrya*' (*agni*) in the sky as energy is made. The three principles which emerge from the single notion of *bīja* are process, organic interconnectedness of the parts and the whole, and a continuous but well-defined course of growth, decay and renewal. The complementariness of matter' and 'energy', indeed, even the trans-substantiation of matter into energy and vice-versa, is implicit in these metaphors.

From the *Ṛgveda* to the later *Tantras*, the concept of 'seed' (*bīja*) is central to both speculative thought, the sciences and the arts. Bharata accepts and assimilates the 'concept' as a central principle of his theory of 'aesthetics', as also an enunciation of the 'process' of artistic expression and communication.* The inter-relatedness and inter-dependence of the parts and the whole of seeding and fruition is basic to his argument. The theatrical experience emerges from a 'seed' (*bīja*)—a term used in the context of the relationship of *rasa* and *bhāva*, as also the structuring of drama, i.e. *itivṛtta* (plot). In the case of the first, Bharata says, 'Just as a tree grows from a seed, and flowers and fruits (including the seed) from a tree, so the sentiments (*rasas*) are the source (root) of all the states (*bhāva*) and likewise the states exist as the source of all the sentiments (*rasa*) (N.S.VI–38). The second, i.e. the concept of *bīja* (seed) in the structure, we shall elaborate later. The use of the 'term' as metaphor clearly echoes Upaniṣadic thought. In the *Nāṭyaśāstra* it takes many shapes and forms as a tree, its branches, leaves, flowers and fruits. The metaphor, not to be extended literally, is an invisible but real foundation of the text. 'Theatre' is an organism, just as life is an organism.

The concept of '*bīja*'[2] has further to be placed within the broader framework of the concept of man and universe or what we today understand as man and nature. The world is a configuration of the five primary elements of earth, water, fire, air and space (*ākāśa*). The inanimate world and the animate world are manifestations of the primary elements. The geological, botanical, zoological and human worlds are interconnected. Flora, fauna, vegetative life, the animal world and the human are but diverse manifestations and forms. Man is no different and is one amongst all life-phenomena. His distinctiveness lies in his capacity of reflection and above all, speech (*vāk*), with

* The word 'theory' is being used with all the provisos mentioned in the previous chapter.

which he is empowered, but qualitatively he is no different than any other form of life (*jīva*). Ecological balance and equilibrium has to be maintained and sustained between the inanimate (*jaḍa*) and animate (*cetana*) worlds, as also amongst the different members of the animate world. The core principles of *ātman* and *brahman*, of *aṇḍa* and *brahmāṇḍa*, of the micro and the macro, are almost a logical corollary of the notion that 'life' in all forms of life is to be equally respected and recognized. The Vedas and the Upaniṣads are replete with discussions on the core concept of *ātman* and *brahman* as the micro and macro levels of the life-phenomenon. We are not alluding at this stage to their interpretation in schools of philosophy.

Closely related and almost a part of the comprehension of the universe as originating from the cosmic egg (*aṇḍa*) and floating on the eternal waters is the concept of '*puruṣa*'. Now, we have a concept of structure for comprehending the universe. The understanding of life in all its diversity is the background for placing the concept of '*puruṣa*' as a central principle. The *Ṛgveda* (*Puruṣa sūkta*) gives a vivid account of the cosmic man and lays the foundation for comprehending the 'human', the anatomical and physiological, physical, social and cosmic man. 'Man', cosmic or human, has a defined structure with the parts and the whole again inter-related and interlocked. The metaphor of the world and society as '*puruṣa*'[3] has to be comprehended as a term of the 'structure' of the different parts interlocked and interdependent. The *yajña* is the ritual enactment of both cosmic and primordial man, as dismemberment and rememberment of the parts and the whole. This is the meaning of the sacrifice of *prajāpati*.

The *bīja* (seed) gives rise to a 'tree', a pole, which signifies verticality. The concept of *puruṣa* is overlayered on it and so the *puruṣa* or image of man also suggests verticality. He too, like the tree, the cosmic pillar, connects the earth and heaven. Like the biological world, he too is born from the cosmic egg—the seed or *bīja*. However, he is both mortal and immortal, the created and creator, micro and macro, physical and paradigmatical: 'The Moon is born from His mind; the Sun from His eyes, Indra and Fire from His mouth; Wind from His breath; the Sky from His navel; the Heaven from His head; the Earth from His feet; the four quarters, from His ear; thus the World was fashioned.' (*Puruṣa sūkta*, RV X.90). The elements—the sun and the moon—constitute this cosmic man who in turn, symbolizes them in micro-form. The human form is in the micro-*puruṣa* with an analogous structure. He too comprises *ātman* and *śarīra* (soul and body).

The *Nāṭyaśāstra* does not refer to either *puruṣa* or to the elements explicitly. However, a close reading of the text makes it clear that the structure of 'drama' is in itself a *puruṣa*, a structure of different parts and limbs where each part is related to the whole. The physical, psychical, individual, social, horizontal and vertical dimensions are interconnected. It is the concept of *puruṣa* along with the other two components of *śarīra* and *ātman* which accounts for a very distinctive attitude to the body, sense perceptions, emotive states and consciousness.

The *Taittirīya Āranyaka* speaks of the creator as moving within the womb of the cosmos, then the unborn is born manifold. In the *Atharvaveda* the seer Nārāyaṇa (AV X.2.) asks the question: 'What is the origin of cosmic creation, the coordination of the human limbs and sense perceptions and mental activities? Who created in them the red fluid that flows like a river? Who put life into them? Who endowed him with seed to perpetuate his life?' Part of the answer given is: 'The *Brahman* manifesting himself as man is the creator of man in the world and man who is embodied *Brahman* has transformed himself in all this . . . . The brain (*medhā*) is called the reservoir of *Brahman,* the human body is the citadel of man. Because *Brahman* resides in this citadel of the human body, it is called *puruṣa* (man)' (AV X.2).

This man has a 'centre' physiologically and organically. The navel, *nābhi,* is the central point. The *garbha* or womb is the unmanifest source of creation and reproduction from where life emerges as from the *bīja* (seed). The three concepts *bīja, nābhi* and *garbha* converge, are overlayered and interpenetrate, to provide the single principle of 'centrality' and an inner invisible core which is unmanifest but which manifests itself in multiform. When it takes 'form', abstract or concrete, it is a *bindu* (drop), with the aspect of stasis and dynamism in-built. As drop of water it spreads. As geometrical form it is point, almost dimensionless point, it holds the structure of any form and shape together.

Other concepts and key words can be identified which permeate the discussion on life-phenomenon. In turn, they provide the concurrent layers and metaphors of Indian art. We have elucidated on seven principal layers and metaphors of Indian art elsewhere.[4] Here, our purpose is to draw attention to a few that Bharata adopts and employs consistently in his text. They denote both process and structure. Foremost amongst these are the principles of centrality and verticality of organic process and of structure through the inter-related concepts of *bīja* and *purusa* along with womb (*garbha*). The concept of *bindu* gives him scope to develop his notions of horizontal spread and basic design of structure with a point and constantly enlarging areas in terms of concentric circles. Bharata adopts these concepts to describe the relationship of the 'incipient' invisible and the explicit form (e.g., context of *bhāva* and *rasa*), or to suggest the relationship of the parts and the whole, or to identify the principal joints of his structure. The 'body' (*śarīra, tanu* and several other words are used) is a primary tool. It is also a term of reference. Physically, it is made up of bones, joints, muscles. The sense organs and sense perceptions are potent vehicles of feeling and sensibility. The body and the mind are interdependent, mutually effecting and affective. Intellection is important, but senses, feeling and sensibility are fundamental. Several key concepts in the *Nāṭyaśāstra* can be comprehended only if we realize that Bharata was adopting and accepting a very different view of the body (*śarīra*) than what is understood as corporeal frame or fleshy mass. Also, he had fully internalized the discourse on the senses and sense perceptions as articulated in the Upaniṣads. Bharata is, without doubt, indebted to the Upaniṣads for the special place given to the outer and inner senses, known by the generic word *indriya.*

A re-reading of the Upaniṣads is convincing proof of the concrete imagery of the senses, the sense perceptions and sense objects of these highly abstract metaphysical texts. The *Kenopaniṣad,* while urging the pupil to go and seek 'beyond the reach of the eye, the ear, speech, touch, smell, etc.', describes the absolute *brahman* as 'the ear of the ear, the mind of the mind, speech of the speech, life of the life (breath), the eye of the eye and yet beyond all these'. The dialogue revolves around the relationship of the senses and mind, the capacity of each to move inward and enlarge outward. Brahman itself is formless and unmanifest; it is only accessible and experienced by means of the senses and the 'mind' The consciousness that the unmanifest (*avyakta*), is experienced and manifested through the senses, shining forth in an instant and disappearing like the twinkling of a star. The *Kaṭhopaniṣad* expands the idea further, by setting up a hierarchy: 'Higher than the senses (and their objects) is the mind; more excellent than the mind (*manas*), the intellect (*sattvam*); above the intellect soars the great soul (*mahātman*) and higher than the great soul (*mahātman*) is the unmanifest (*avyakta*); and higher than the unmanifested is the Supreme Soul (*puruṣa* here, could also be Brahman)'—(*Kaṭhopaniṣad, Valli* III, Verses 10–11). The *Upaniṣad,* considered the most refined statement of a world-view and speculation on the nature of the universe and the life of man, makes it clear that this was not a life-denying world view. It was one which was conscious of the process of gradual refinement from one plane to the other and the need for restraint and discipline (*sādhanā* and *tapas*)

Bharata's adherence and debt to this world-view is clear when he repeatedly speaks of the 'eye' and the 'ear' and purification. It is not only ritual purification; it is the constant endeavour to arrive at a greater and greater degree of subtlety and refinement. The theatrical universe is the world of the 'audible' and the 'visible'. The senses and sense-organs and perceptions play a crucial role in the evolution of the theory, as also the techniques of each of the four instrumentalities of expression—sound, word (*vācika*) and body language (*āṅgika*), décor and dress, (*āhārya*) internal states (*sāttvika*). However, as in the case of the Upaniṣads, although the senses are primary and as indispensable as horses in a chariot, they must be disciplined, restrained and groomed. In the Upaniṣads the mind and the intellect were the charioteers. Here, the initial discipline of the artist-creator is necessary for the probability and possibility of a total experience. If in discursive thought, the mind and intellect play a regulating role, here, the refinement of feeling and sensibility is crucial. Harnessing of the capacity of the senses for outward and inward reach is the discipline and austerity demanded. It is only then that the artist can have the ability to turn the 'senses'—outward and inward. The introduction of the concept of *yoga* in the world of theatre assumes significance when seen within the framework of a world-view where equilibrium, balance and harmony of the physical, sensuous, emotive, intellectual and spiritual levels is considered essential. *Yoga* is the *yoking* and joining of these levels in an ascending order—a movement from the physical to the metaphysical. The *Nāṭyaśāstra* implies, although it does not explicitly state, a theory of aesthetics. Explicitly, Bharata speaks of artistic expression and communication. The concept of *rasa* cannot be understood fully without taking into account the larger background of the speculative thought of the Upaniṣads.

Without explicitly stating it, Bharata makes it clear that what he has set out to do is to present a universe of name and form (*nāma* and *rūpa*) of the physical, the mortal, of the body, senses and speech (*vāk*), which will match speculation and meditation, ritual and sacrifice. In fact, he does make an explicit statement at the very end of his work:

> He who always hears the reading of that (*śāstras*) which is auspicious, sportful, originating from Brahman's mouth, very holy, pure, good, destructive of sins and who puts into practice and witnesses carefully the performance (drama, we may add the word 'artistic') will attain the same blessed goal which masters of Vedic knowledge and performers of sacrifice (ritual *pūjā*)—attain (XXXVI 77–79).

This, read along with what we have pointed out in an earlier chapter regarding the necessity of discipline (*sādhana*, even *tapas*) in the artistic act, will make it clear that what Bharata has set out to do is to use the very language and vocabulary of name and form (*nāma* and *rūpa*—of identity and specificity of form) to evoke that which is beyond form or without form (*parārūpa*), and all this through the vehicle of the senses and sense perceptions and feeling, not intellection.

At the level of structure, Bharata creates an analogue to the physical layout of *yajña*. Just as in a *śālā*, altars (*vedis*) of different sizes and shapes are built, there is both concurrent and sequential action, and multiple media are employed—all for the purpose of replicating the cosmos' and correcting the cosmic time and calendar, the *Nāṭya-śāstra* and its varied chapters with divisions and components are the ritual altars of this grand and complex design. The dramatic spectacle, like the *yajña*, has a moral and ethical purpose. It will conduce moral duty (*dharma*), wealth economic well-being (*artha*), refine sensibilities (*kāma*) and lead to liberation (*mokṣa*). The arts are thus an alternate, if not a parallel, path for the avowed goals of a culture which move concurrently on the three levels of the *ādhibhautika* (material), *ādhyātmika* (individual soul and self) and *ādhidaivika* (metaphysical divine). The multidimensional nature is evident, even if not explicitly stated.

Chapters I and II of the *Nāṭyaśāstra* lay down, in unambiguous though veiled terms, the foundations of this structure. Bharata internalizes, incorporates the Upaniṣadic world-view at the level of concepts and the ultimate goal of the artistic experience and creates a structure which is an analogue to brāhmaṇical ritual (*yajña*). However, since Bharata does not make explicit the foundational design of his citadel of drama and all this is suggested, implied, even deliberately veiled (*guha*), as he says in the end, the text has given rise to a vast number of interpretations and commentaries. This also explains, in part, why both commentators and contemporary scholars focussed attention on particular aspects or portions or even certain verses of the text, and not on its unseen, but very real and deep foundations of a distinctive world-view and its chiselled language of articulation. There is the implicit flow of 'concepts' and attitudes like an *anth-salilā* (unseen river, Sarasvatī) which provides the integral vision to the text.

Explicitly, the *Nāṭyaśāstra*, no doubt, is divided into thirty-six chapters and has a sequence. The structure of the text can be restated in terms of the concern of the author to present all levels of the artistic experience, forms of expression, nature and levels of response. He does not restrict himself either to a discussion on the nature of the artistic experience or only to the technical details of each media or genre of expression.

The thirty-six chapters of the *Nāṭyaśāstra* can be regrouped from the point of view of (i) artistic experience; (ii) the artistic content or states of being, the modes of expression through word, sound, gesture, dress, decorations and methods of establishing correspondences between physical movement, speech and psychical states, as also communication and reception by the audience, readers; and (iii) structure of the dramatic form, popularly translated as 'plot'. The *itivṛtta* is, however, a more comprehensive term for both structure and phasing.

(i) The artistic experience is viewed from the point of view of the creator—poet, writer, artist, painter, architect, and interpreter—in this case, the actor, the singer, the executor of the architectural design, as also the spectator and receiver. The artistic experience is acausal and whole, a state of beatitude and bliss in the mind of the experiencer, the creator. It is subsequently transferred, translated through either the media (e.g., words, paint, sound), or through indeed another person (i.e. actor and characters of drama). A reading of the *Nāṭyaśāstra* especially the sixth and seventh chapters, makes it very clear that although Bharata appears to be speaking only about artistic expression and methodologies for evoking response and resonance, he was indeed conscious of these distinctions. After all, who was conceiving and visualizing before form came into being? An experience of undifferentiation, of a state of (concentration) *samādhi*, an acausal, a-intellected state, intuitive and non-cognitive, alone could be liberated from immediacy and boundaries. This could make it possible or probable for creation to take place. Whether stated in words or not, it is '*rasa*' in the singular, the highly charged state of momentary freedom and emancipation which motivates, inspires creation. Distancing, *taṭastha*, is consistently implied and is an underlying tenet of the *Nāṭyaśāstra*. Exactly as in poetry, music, dance and the visual arts, the 'unsaid' silent is almost more important than the 'said' and 'sung'. Here also it is the most important implicit level which is not explicated.

(ii) It is this experience which facilitates an abstraction of life into its primary emotions and sentiments. The specificity of the individual, the emotive particularity is secondary, for each is but a carrier of the primary abstracted state of love or hatred, etc. These, then are the content of art, known by their familiar terms, the eight or nine *rasas* and their expression as dominant states, *sthāyi bhāvas*. The two levels of the undifferentiated state of oneness, non-duality, and the differentiated states of diversity and multiplicity are connected. The establishment of a system of correspondences between specific emotive states (*sthāyi bhāvas*) and the media (speech, body language, sound, music) on the one hand, and the character types, social class, on the other, is logical. This is another fundamental level of the work.

(iii) The third level is the potential of the artistic work, through the specificity of content and form and the variations to evoke a similar, if not identical, undifferentiated state of release and emancipation (*svātantrya*) in the spectator and reader from the immediate so-muchness of life (*iyattā*).

On this conceptual foundation, the physical structure of the theatre is created. Chapter II deals with the actual construction of the theatre, the different types and the shapes and sizes of the theatre. Now, just as at the conceptual level, a micro-model is created with the Upaniṣads as the source, the physical theatre, the stage and the audience area is also a micro-model of the cosmos. The consecration of the site, the laying of the foundation of the theatre, the construction of the stage, the division into central and peripheral areas and identification of a centre (*brahmasthāna*), the placement of deities of the directions are a replication. It is a micro-model of the cosmos. The physical place replicates cosmic space. Theatre and the stage in particular is an analogue of the ritual space of the *yajña.* The *śālā,* the *vedis,* the altars, were the components of the *yajña.* On the stage, the central and peripheral areas, serve the same purpose. Brahmā is the principle of centrality and verticality. Others take their places. Bharata asserts very early in the text that all the orders of space (*triloka*) and the seven divisions (continents) and seas will be included. The physical space of the theatre thus is a neutral performative space with the potential of being transformed into space of any order.

Some scholars have suggested that there is no unity and logical progression between chapters I and II. Kuiper[5] even suggests that Chapter II is a later addition. If we read these chapters as Bharata's attempt to lay the conceptual and physical foundations of his scheme, the two are interconnected. The first alludes through the language of myth, the inspiration for his work and the origin of drama. The entire mythical world of Brahman, Śiva, Indra, Sarasvatī, Viṣṇu, Śeṣa the great serpent, the Daityas, Bhūtas, Yakṣas, Piśācas and Guhyakas, are participators as 'actors', protagonists or agitators or protectors. This is the world of the imagination, of the celestial and terrestrial, but not actual. If Indra is empowered as 'hero', Sarasvatī is 'heroine'. She is *vāk,* the embodiment of 'speech' (I.96-97) and Śiva assumes a special role of an energizer. After the Cosmos has been replicated, Bharata conjures up the cosmic nature of the world of creativity where the *devas* and *asuras* meet in friendly combat and where poetic justice is demanded for all. The first chapter has drawn the attention of scholars—for trying to trace the historical origins of Indian drama. Perhaps, it should be looked at as a most charming and delightful narration of the fulsome, joyful world of 'creativity' and imagination. Commitment to only a single source or cult or affiliation or 'ideology' is not required.

It is this world of creativity and imagination which has to be given a physical space. It can be 'open', but has to be protected. In both cases the *jarjara* (the pole) is basic. Chapter II provides the physical space.[6]

The chapters which follow, namely, chapters III, IV and V, are closely linked. Bharata had begun with the conceptual, mythical and physical space in chapters I and II. Chapter III is the methodology of consecrating the physical space so created so that for the time and duration the space is now a sacralized cosmic space. It is, therefore, necessary to have *pūjā*. Consecration of physical space is 'universal' whether it is *yajña* or temple, *stūpa*, church or mosque, popular ritual, open doors or indoors. The rituals of all societies, the Yorubas, American Indians and countless groups in India, are living testimony. Bharata only lays down the broad parameters of the methodology of 'replicating' the 'cosmos' in defined finite space and time, so that in turn it can be the vehicle and instrumentality of suggesting the transphysical, as also specified 'space' and 'time'. Again, in this field scholars have attempted to track down the origins to Aryan or Dravidian sources rather than identifying Bharata's clear intent and purpose in devoting a whole chapter to *pūjā*. He is not creating religious drama of a particular class, caste or denomination. He is consecrating space which would prepare actors, performers and audience to be transported to the world of the imagination and simultaneously to the divine and the heavenly. The celestial and the terrestrial are being interconnected. In the language of the Romantics, he is preparing the 'actors' and the audience for 'a willing suspension of belief' in the drama which is to follow.

Just as through the *pūjā* all deities, directions and quarters were being established so as to locate the specific within the universal and cosmic, so in chapters IV and V Bharata suggests the methodologies of preparing participants and audience to link different orders of time and space.

Chapter IV begins by an engaging anecdote of Śiva's pleasure at seeing the performance of the first play (*Amṛtamanthana samavakāra*). It is Śiva who suggests to Bharata that he could profitably use the cadences of movement, called *karaṇas* in the preliminaries of the play. Thereafter follows the long description of a category of movements, called *karaṇas* and *aṅgahāras* and their composition in choreographical patterns, called *piṇḍibandha*. Bharata accepts this because it would, once again, facilitate inner and outer preparation. Pure dance and movement would be the best vehicle of creating an atmosphere in the nature of an 'overture'. Without content, meaning, theme pleasing and delightful, these sequences could replicate the cosmic dance of Śiva in its infinite variety. For the dance of Śiva is in no-time, he dances in the cosmos. The legend alludes both to the divine origin of dance (*nṛtta*) as a category and to its place within the theatrical spectacle. Also, different orders of time, the 'cosmic' time, 'no-time' of Śiva's dance and the limited time of the performance of the *karaṇas* and *aṅgahāras* is suggested. All this is non-content and narrative, and as such an appropriate preparation for being transported to another order of time and space. At the level of technique, Bharata introduces compositions of movement before speaking about techniques of body. He elaborates on this in chapters VIII to XI.

Replication and remodelling is the essence of chapters III and IV, till we arrive at chapter V where Bharata now systematically lays down the multiple levels of his operation. The movement from the celestial to the terrestrial, from the divine to the human, from the austere ritual of the *bhṛṅgāra* and *jarjara* to humour and play, from the communication with the king and ruler to the lay, young and old in the audience is described. It is in chapter V that Bharata unfolds his larger structure in miniscule. The *pūrvaraṅga* is a 'code' to establish different orders of 'time' and 'space' of the three dimensions of dialogue through the three 'actors' who enter and exit repeatedly in five phases to establish, each time, another order of space and time. The transformative character of 'theatre', of the stage, and the role of the actor to perform and communicate at multiple levels to a variety of audiences, is now made explicit. A fuller analysis of the importance of the *pūrvaraṅga* has been made elsewhere.[7] Bharata may not have revealed his foundational plan at the level of concept, but the ground plan at the level of concrete form he makes evident. The *pūrvaraṅga* is the well laid-out ground plan of his schema on which the theatrical edifice will be constructed. He is, as it were, announcing that drama will move at multiple levels of space and time, concurrently.

Having laid out the parameters, Bharata almost jumps into the 'core' of his work. So what will be presented? What is the creative process which will make it possible? What will it represent and how will it be represented and how will he communicate? The famous chapters VI and VII on *rasa, sthāyi bhāva* have captured the imagination of the theoretician and practitioner alike, for centuries. India presents a unique phenomenon of an unbroken continuity with this 'source'; the 'concept' of *rasa, sthāyi bhāva* and *vyabhicāri bhāvas* along with the dictum, now almost a cliche, of '*vibhāvānubhāva-vyabhicāri-saṁyogād rasaniṣpattiḥ*' (VI–31).

The abstraction of 'life' into primary moods, sentiments, primary emotive states, is basic and universal to the human. It is not culture specific or individual or particular. Yes, the culture specific, the individual or society are embodiments of the universal human psychical states. The primary human emotions are expressed in a variety of ways; indeed, an infinite variety in time, space and locale through distinctive modes of speech, body language and gesticulation, dress and costume, but love and laughter, jealousy, fear and wonder are universal. It is these 'universals' which are common that constitute the core 'theme' They have determinates and stimulants *vibhāva* and *anubhāva*. Through the interpenetration of particular *rasas* and *sthāyi bhāvas* and their coming together (*saṁyoga*) a state of *rasa* (*niṣpatti*) is evoked or created. Its final relish (*āsvāda*) is comparable to the taste or after-taste of a good meal with many flavours (*vyañjana*) when specificity is lost but the experience of a good meal or a sense of relish remains. This is what drama or all creativity explores, sheer joy or pleasure, pain or pathos, wonder or amazement, and their mutual interplay. Bharata explores, investigates these with the finesse of a 'psychic' physician and the mastery of a skilled craftsman, better, with an artificial intelligence, as a knowledge expert, to lay down 'rules' and programmes for simulating the 'phenomenon' of psychic states and their manifestation through speech, body language, dress, costumes, etc.

Having dwelt on 'origin', preparation, intent and the non-individualized, almost abstract content (*rasa bhāva*), the artistic inspiration and process of impersonalization from chapter VIII onwards, Bharata's concern is with the formal values of the art, 'technique' and systems of communication and ıesponse. These chapters largely, not wholly, are the explicit dimension ot his text.

Logically, he begins with the analysis of the body—the motor and sensory system. Anatomy, especially the joints rather than the musculature, is his concern. That he understands the nervous system is obvious from his enumeration of physical stimulus and psychic response, psychic states and expression through physical movement. The *āṅgikābhinaya* chapters of the *Nāṭyaśāstra* have to be understood as body-language in contemporary language and not merely as gesticulation, poses and postures, as has often been done. There is a cluster of chapters which deal with the subject and the role of body-language in theatre is integral to his intent and purpose. It is not 'auxiliary', as has been suggested by both medieval commentators as also some modern scholars. These chapters include a wide range of subjects. He begins by breaking up the anatomical structure into its principal parts—the head, trunk, pelvis and the upper and lower limbs. Bharata explores the possibility of physical motor movement of each part. He is exact and precise, anatomically and physiologically. These he terms as *aṅga* and *upāṅga*, normally translated as major and minor limbs. In fact, what he is doing is to take the head and face as a unit and then analysing all possibilities of movement of the particular part from the eyes, eyebrows, eyelids, pupils to the whole eye (*dṛṣṭi*), nose, cheeks, upper and lower chin, mouth, colour of face and the neck. Everything above the first and second vertebrae (the atlas and axis) of the spine has been taken into account, except the ears (chapter VIII, M.M. Ghosh edition). Next, he applies the same technique to the 'hand' and 'hands', as one unit comprising the wrist joint, palm and fingers. The underlying understanding of the joints, carpals, metacarpals and phalanges is exact and comprehensive. It is from the physical understanding that he devises a whole sub-system of hand positions and movements (i.e. wrist, palm and fingers) called *hastas*.

Thereafter, he explores direction, height, movements (including the arms) away from the body and towards the body. Just as in the case of the head and face, the first and second vertebrae were the cut-off points, so here, too the ball-and-socket joint of the shoulder, the hinge joint of the elbows and wrist joint are points of articulation (chapter IX). The same principle is followed in the third group, comprising parts of the trunk, pelvis and the lower limbs including the feet (chapter X). Each single part of the body and its possibility of movement is then co-related with its potential for giving expression to a particular emotion or state. Bharata does not forget that the body is capable of moving gracefully, beautifully, without meaning and import, and thus in the case of movements of the hands and the lower limbs he speaks also of pure movement (*nṛtta*). The word he uses for the dimension of applicability is important. He adopts the term *viniyoga* (methodology) from Vedic ritual and applies it uniformly in his enumeration of *āṅgikābhinaya* (to express, to communicate, to reach out through the *aṅgas-śarīra*).

Having explored the different parts, he goes on to provide a broad spectrum of movement techniques where the whole body is employed. Basic to the system is training of the body. Without *vyāyāma* (exercise) and proper health and nourishment, nothing is possible (chapter XI). The connection between Bharata's system of exercise and what we today recognize as *haṭhayoga* on the one hand, and martial arts, on the other, is more than obvious. Equilibrium and equibalance and holding of the spine with equiweight is suggested by the two seminal terms, *sama* and *sauṣṭhava.* These terms, as we shall see later, are applied to the spheres of music and language. Units of movement emerge from this control of the body in sitting, standing and reclining positions. The *sthānas, āsanas* and *maṇḍalas* are basic stylized first positions, static positions of standing, sitting and knee bends (plie) from which a variety of movement possibilities emerge. The *cārī* (walking or moving) is the first of these movements. The foot-contact and relative distribution of weight on-the-ground and off-the-ground is suggested by the descriptive terms *bhaumī* and *ākāśikī* (air-sky) *cārīs* (chapters X and XII). The *cārī* (walking movements, as physical possibility of the lower limbs), are then transformed into the conventional typologies of gaits. This is the level of applicability in drama. The gaits (*gati*) are related to character-types, to moods and sentiments, and can be in different tempos. Bharata provides a staggering repertoire of sitting postures and gaits to suit gender, character, occasion, mood and dramatic situation (chapter XIII). The *cāris* are also the basic unit of movement for the cadences of movement called *karaṇas* and *aṅgahāras*. These Bharata had described in chapter IV. At the level of technique, these can only be comprehended or vaguely reconstructed through a proper and comprehensive competence in the techniques outlined in chapters VIII to XI. In an earlier work, a fuller analysis of the *āṅgika* has been attempted.[8]

At this point Bharata takes a pause, as if to state and remind the reader that the framework of his analysis is the 'stage' and its transformative character. Chapter II had dwelt on the theatre-types, the areas of the stage, the principal divisions into the front and backstage, the central and peripheral areas, the backstage and the audience areas. Now, he returns to this at another level. The stage is his focus. This is the limited defined space. We learn of the placement of the drums, the musical ensemble (*kutapa*) and how this physical stage will become an analogue of the cosmic space, or at least concurrently be the replication of the abode of the gods and men (*daivika* and *mānuṣī*), the miniscule of India (Bhāratavarṣa) and its different cultural regions. A basic spatial grid is devised which makes it possible to transform a single physical area into the three spaces of water, earth and sky, diverse regions, different 'locales' of 'outside', 'inside', 'proximity' and 'distance'. Chapter XIV on *kakṣāvibhāga* and *pravṛtti* is Bharata's devise and mechanism for encompassing all orders of 'space'. The chapter is important also because it touches upon concepts of style (*vṛtti*), regional schools (*pravṛtti*), as also of the two modes of delivery of movement and speech, namely, *nāṭyadharmī* and *lokadharmī*. He had introduced these concepts in chapter VI, v.23–26. The cluster of the four notions of *kakṣāvibhāga* (zonal divisions), styles (*vṛttis*), regional characteristics (or schools) (*pravṛttis*), the two modes—sophisticated or stylized and a more natural mode (*nāṭya* and *lokadharmī*) —of delivery of movement and speech, along with energetic and delicate (*tāṇḍava* and *sukumāra*) modes as also *daivika* (divine) and *mānuṣī* (human) (chapter XIII, 28) levels, provides an invaluable cluster of principles which guide not only physical movement (*āṅgika*), which he has described earlier, but also what is to follow later in the group of chapters which deal with the other two *abhinayas* (out of his four of *āṅgika, vācika, āhārya* and *sāttvika*), namely the *vācika* and *āhārya*. In each of these spheres of sound, speech and music, as also in the matter of costumes, coiffure, there are and can be special styles of presentation and an attempt at localizing or specifying speech, movement, music and dress. The nature of presentation can be soft, lyrical or strong stylized or natural, grand elevated or earthly, divine or human. Appropriately, he places this crucial chapter at this stage of his work before elaborating on the other principal tools of creativity, sound, word, speech and prosody. Also, it is the reading of this chapter which makes it explicit that Bharata's sense of 'time' and 'place' could not possibly have followed the Aristotelian unities of 'time' and 'place'. As a principle of the structure of drama and its framework with a distinctly different paradigm all that we understand from either Greek drama or realistic theatre of the nineteenth century can be discerned here.

However, to move on to Bharata's next concern, 'word' and 'speech', he devotes four long chapters to the strictly *vācika* (chapters XV to XIX). For him the *vācika* (articulated word) is the body (*tanu*) of drama. The primacy of the word is asserted in unambiguous terms: 'In this world (lit. here) the *śāstras* are made up of words, rests on words: hence there is nothing beyond words, and words are at the source of everything' (chapter XV, verse 3, M.M.Ghosh edition).

The articulated word (*pāṭhya*), he divides into two, Sanskrit and Prakrit. Thereafter, there is a minute analysis, as in the case of the body-system, of first, the principal units of structure, nouns, verbs, particles, propositions, nominal suffixes, compound words, euphonic combinations (*sandhi*) and case-endings. Then follows the further break-up into vowels and consonants, words, verse and prose, metre and rhythm, syllables (long and short, heavy and light), rhyme and feet in couplet. The units of language at their primary level are all taken care of. The method is the same as in the description of the parts of the human body. Chapter XV stops short at metrical patterns, to which Bharata devotes a separate chapter (chapter XVI). Chapter XV, called *Chandovidhāna,* is distinguished from that on metrical pattern, called *Vṛttalakṣaṇa* (chapter XVI); the titles are explicit statements on how he is proceeding. In the chapter on metrical patterns, Bharata cites many examples which exhibit his knowledge of and familiarity with versification. His corpus of information on the subject is impressive. Many fascinating myths are contained in the verses. The variety of metrical patterns is vast. Their names cover all aspects of nature. The character of the flora and fauna inspires the shape and form of the metres. This was also so in the case of the *karaṇas,* e.g. *hariṇapluta, mayūra-lalita,* etc. Logically, these two are followed by chapters on diction (*lakṣaṇa*) and its thirty-six varieties. The word *lakṣaṇa* itself has many layers of meaning and several connotations. The word has been variously translated as 'hallmark', 'indicator', 'signifier', etc.[9] Each is now related to the context and field of usage and applicability. Metre, rhyme, diction are all related to the mood or sentiment (*rasa*) and should be so appropriately employed (chapter XVII, 42). Thereatter follows an analysis of figures of speech, principally simile (*upamā*), metaphor (*rūpaka*), condensed expression (*dīpaka*) and *yamaka.* After delineating upon the sub-categories of each, Bharata has an interesting section on the defects (*doṣa*) of various types, as also the merits or *guṇas* of speech and metrical patterns. The purpose of it all is no doubt to convey the moods and sentiments (*rasa*), and present the emotive states. Bharata is fully conscious of the power of the 'word' and its effect on the listener. Agreeable and appropriate words in a play 'are like the adornment (*alaṁkāra*) of swans on a lotus lake; inappropriate ones have the incongruity of a pair of courtesan and an ascetic brāhmaṇa.' These chapters have been the bedrock of subsequent theories of rhetorics and poetics in Sanskrit. A torrential stream, almost a river of *alaṁkāra śāstra* flows out of these chapters. So much significance has been laid on them, that little needs to be added. For our purpose this brief enumeration was necessary to adequately identify the primary role of word and diction in Bharata's scheme of an inter-related world of the four *abhinayas.*

Chapter XVIII is devoted to languages, especially recitation in Prākṛt and the use of different dialects. This chapter has to be seen in relation to Bharata's principles of the regional schools (*pravṛttis*), styles (*vṛttis*) and sophisticated and natural modes (*nāṭya* and *lokadharmī*) enumerated in chapter XIII. Bharata makes a valiant effort to be comprehensive in his treatment. However, he is aware that all rules of specificity can only be exemplary and not rigidly prescriptive. Appropriately, he ends the chapter by leaving the door open: 'These are guidelines (*vidhāna*) which may be used for employing languages and dialects in dramas. However, whatever has been omitted can be included by observing the world and humanity (*loka*) or literally that which wise gather from local usage' (chapter XVIII, verse 61). Bharata is obviously all too conscious of the limitless variety and the possibility of change, and thus, in the matter of language and dress, he displays an open, flexible approach. Chapter XIX limits itself to modes of address and intonation. While the description of modes of address provides an insight into human interaction and social status, an interesting part of this chapter is the section on intonation and recitation and Bharata's relating the use of specific notes to particular moods/sentiments and his identification of the three voice registers (*sthāna*); the breast (*uras*), throat (*kaṇṭha*) and head (*śiras*). Three pitches emerge from the three registers and the relative ascending and descending orders are indicated. Once again a full acquaintance with techniques of voice production from different centres of the body is obvious. Bharata refers to the four accents (*udātta*), grave (*anudātta*), circumflex (*svarita*) and quivering (*kampita*). Again, he relates them to specific sentiments and moods. This group then constitutes the basis of the six *alaṁkāras* of the recitative modes which can be high or low, excited or grave, fast or slow. The purpose of introducing the basic components of 'notes', 'registers', pitches and tempo at this stage is, obviously, two-fold. One, to relate them to the specific sentiments/moods (*rasa*), and the other, to prepare his reader for a detailed enumeration on music (*saṅgīta*) which follows much later. Bharata uses this device of introducing a subject, in a nutshell, in a particular context (e.g., *vṛttis* and *dharmis* in the context of *rasa* and *sthāyi bhāva* as also the *kakṣāvibhāga* and elaboration later in chapter XXIII) and then taking up the subject later for a fuller analysis. This structural format is evident in respect of many subjects. In this context, he is situating the articulated sound-note (*svara*) and word both within the field of poetry and drama as also making a link with the chapters on music, which come much later. He is conscious of both the intrinsic inter-relatedness of each medium as also its autonomy. This was obvious in the case of the category of *nṛtta* as dance and then in relation to both poetry and music.

In characteristic style, just as he had paused to speak of *kakṣāvibhāga* (zonal divisions) after the *āṅgika* chapters, he now pauses to give attention to structure, proper. Having dwelt on the primacy of sound and word, body language and gestures, the principles of transformation of physical space, he turns to 'time' and movement of drama. This is the structural elevation plan of his design. Now formal aspects of types of structures and within the types, the movement of 'time' as 'plot' of each of these structures is described. Appropriately, they are called *daśarūpa-lakṣaṇaṁ* and *itivṛtta* (chapters XX and XXI). While the first (chapter XX) presents a typology of plays and their chief characteristics, the second (chapter XXI) goes into the 'core' of Bharata's conception of the theatrical structure. This moves not in an ascending line of beginning, conflict, climax and denouement, but in a circular fashion with a series of concentric circles, all overlayered and connected to each other through the concept of *bīja* (seed), suggesting organic growth, and *bindu* (drop of a liquid and point or gnomon of early geometry), indicating structure and dimension.

We had referred to these seminal concepts along with *puruṣa* as the pervasive language of pre-Bharata speculative thought, as also the paradigm of *puruṣa* in the brāhmaṇical *yajña*. Bharata assimilates the concepts and uses the terms *bīja* (seed) and *bindu* (point) systematically throughout his text and implies the knowledge of the concept of *puruṣa*. These are the unifying threads of his overall structure.

We will recall that Bharata had used the metaphor of the 'seed', tree and branches in the discussion on moods/sentiments (*rasa*) and emotive states (*sthāyi bhāva*) (chapters VI and VII). He now returns to them even more explicitly while laying out the structural principles of drama.

It is significant that Bharata places the two chapters on types of drama and the structure of plays roughly in the middle of his text. The two chapters link two broad divisions of his text from chapters I to XIX and XXII to XXXVI. In the preceding chapters, he had taken up one set of issues, principally of space and methods of expression through body-language, sound, note and word. In the succeeding chapters, he takes up the other two *abhinayas* (viz. *sāttvika* and *āhārya*), music as a distinct category and those of spectator, audience and other issues of a general type relevant to theatre which permeate all aspects and cannot be restricted only to the tangible structure of drama.

Understandably, this is the stage at which Bharata undertakes to evolve typologies. In chapters XX and XXI he begins first by enumerating typologies of plays (*daśarūpaka*). In the succeeding chapters (XXII, XXIII and XXIV) typologies of styles, heroes, heroines, characters, regional characteristics, types of situations and décor are discussed.

All these are governed by the overall structure of different types of drama. This is the *itivṛtta*, normally translated by the inadequate term 'plot'. The term literally visualizes a circle (*vṛtta*). So, it is, was, or can be, a circle.

This is the defined boundary of structure which is not uni-dimensional. It is multi-dimensional. Within the overall structure there is the possibility of several types of compositions or structures comparable to three dimensional blocks or cubes which can be arranged in different configurations. These govern the dynamics of the movement and the multi- or at least three layers of 'time'. In the chapters on the construction of the theatre (chapter II) and on *kakṣāvibhāga* (chapter XIII) exploration was in space. In chapter V (*pūrvaraṅga*) the multi-levelled 'space' and 'time' was codified through the repetitive entrances and exits of the group of three. Now, Bharata explores 'time' multi-dimensional through a tripartite module of the notions *avasthā, arthaprakṛti* and *sandhi*, employing consistently the metaphor of *bīja* (seed), *bindu* (point) and suggesting *puruṣa* as an unspoken term of reference through the notion of *mukha, pratimukha, garbha,* etc. Medieval commentators from Śrīśaṅkuka to Abhinava, to modern scholars such as, Byrsky[10] in particular, have commented extensively on the concept of the *itivṛtta* as structure and the notions of *bīja* (seed) and *bindu* (point) and their significance. Some attention has also been given by the present author to the concept of the *sandhis.*[11] Nevertheless, some further remarks on the inherent nature of the dramatic structure and the validity of using three different types of time movement concepts, each interlocked, may be pertinent here.

Perhaps, first we may look at the three categories in terms of shape and form because the dramatic structure is the essential *form* (*rūpa*) of drama. Reduced to the geometrical abstract form, the three notions can be represented within the overall area of a circle as

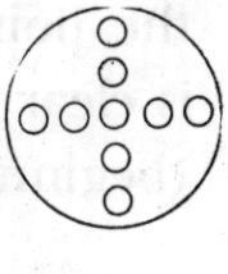

Each time there is movement towards the centre or from the centre to the periphery and the 'centres' of the two types of movement 'converge', even coincide. Further, if each category of *avasthā* (state) *arthaprakṛti* (progression or movement of theme) and *sandhi* (junctures or transitions) is seen as volume or solid mass (*ghana*), further complexity is possible. Finally, if each of these blocks is multilayered (i.e. sets of blocks, one on top of each other, as in a child's game of blocks) and can be joined together in a number of configurations, permutations and combinations, the infinite variety of play which is possible will be more than evident. Modern mathematical blocks as pedagogical aids are well understood. Bharata's system has the enigma of a similar puzzle; it has flexibility and presents challenge. The puzzle can certainly be solved. Many structures, shapes and forms can be created by interlocking the modules in different permutations and combinations. Obviously, the blocks cannot be reduced to a line or placed in a progression of linear arrow time. Linearity is subsumed in the 'model' but is not the totality; the movement is essentially circular.

It was the attempt to apply the yardsticks of linear time scale and 'point' and 'line' in general geometrical terms rather than volume and multi-dimension that in part resulted in the assessment of the Sanskrit dramatic structure by some, if not many, as loose, episodic and unclear. However, leaving aside geometry and the critical debate on the issue, let us return to the three categories of *avasthā, arthaprakṛti* and *sandhis.* Explanatory translations of the three are clear indicators.

In the first, i.e. *avasthā* (states), the movement is from the point of view of the hero, the chief protagonist. This is clear enough in the names of the five stages, i.e. *ārambha* (beginning), *prayatna* (effort), *prāptisambhava* (possibility of attainment), *niyataphalaprāpti* (the possibility of resolution but not of certainty of overcoming of obstacles, conflicts), *phalayoga* or *phalāgama* (fruition). This suggests a clear linear order of progression. Although the stages of *niyati* (determinacy, causal connections) has been long debated, it is clear that the stages are from the point of view of the hero and are moving progressively to a goal. There is a linearity here but it is subsumed in the overall circular structure. Nevertheless, the movement of states of mind and stages of action by a hero cannot constitute the totality of the dramatic structure.

It is here tnat the second and more important dimension of *arthaprakṛti* (nature of the movement of the essential theme) is brought in. Its nature of development is like an organism; it is embedded; it sprouts, grows and there is fruition. Appropriately, the metaphors of *bīja* (seed) and *bindu* (point) are employed. The introduction of the core theme is the seed (*bīja*), its outer structural manifestation is like a drop of liquid or a point (*bindu*). It spreads, enlarges (*vistāra* is Bharata's word) and is present throughout. The theme is made evident as sprout or delicate trunk or visibly flagged *patākā* (in geometry it is the incentre-cum-orthocentre of an equilateral triangle) and meanders through the *prakarī* (that which is thrown about or scattered, the proliferation of branches of a tree) to the final *kārya* (the last stage of action or fruition in the analogy of the tree). If we follow the logic of this division, it would appear that the metaphor of *bīja, bindu, patākā, prakarī* and *kārya* also suggest a horizontal expansion or growth, where at each stage the 'theme', 'core' is present as quintessence. Thus, that which is progressive, linear or even vertical from the point of view of the hero, is pervasive, permeating from the point of view of essential theme.

The third and, in a way, most important is the concept of the *sundhis* (joints, junctures). How are all these elements of progression, permeation and proliferation from the point of view of hero, theme, etc., to be joined together and juxtaposed? This time, the implicit metaphor is that of the *puruṣa* (man) or vaguely, even architecture. The constituents are: *mukha, pratimukha, garbha, vimarśa* or *avamarśa* and *nirvahaṇa.* The literal translation of these terms—mouth, progression (literally counter mouth), womb, pause, or complexity and resolution—will perhaps give us a clue to the nature of the terms employed. The first three are metaphors of the body. The latter two suggest movement. Finding exact English equivalents is not easy. This is loaded terminology which emerges from Bharata's understanding from the body-system as also a familiarity with the methodology, *viniyoga,* of the *yajña.* The analogy of the *itivṛtta* as the *śarīra* (body) at its grossest and subtle levels of drama alludes to the nature of interconnections and the movement of time within the dramatic structure. It is the dynamics of movement and nature of interconnections which are suggested through the terms *mukha, pratimukha* and the more complex but fundamentally germane levels of movement within *garbha* (in the womb—unmanifest but dynamic) to further complexities (*vimarśa*) and again final resolution.

Although conscious of and recognizing the richness and intricacy of debate and discussion on these concepts within the tradition from Abhinavagupta to Sāgaranandin[12] and Bhoja, it was necessary to dwell at some length on the cluster of the three principles, because they constitute the foundational structure of Bharata's text and make clear an integral vision which identifies key concepts. They also employ a set of metaphors consistently throughout his text, which have the legitimacy and validity of a chiselled refinement within the tradition at the level of both speculative thought as also ritual practices and notions derived from geometry, anatomy and physiology. The last two he employs somewhat more precisely than we do today. Often, we observe that the social sciences and humanities employ vocabulary of the 'sciences', physical and natural, and contemporary technology in a vague, generalized way. Bharata exhibits a somewhat deeper understanding, although obviously no specialization. He, too, mixes his metaphors. Nonetheless, his acquaintance with both measure, notions in geometry and of actual 'time' is further borne out by the detailed account of 'time', 'time-measures' in the two chapters. The discussion on the division of day and night, the counts of *muhūrtas, nāḍikās* and many other units in the context of types of plays, seen in the context of the nature of drama and typologies, indicates Bharata's consciousness of actual physical duration—time of the performance, the internal time of the plays (of the progression of character and dramatic action) and a conceptual time where the gods and humans meet. The structure of drama in time has to be seen along with the structure of drama in space: both ascribing to the concurrent multidimensional notion of *triloka* and *trikāla* and, therefore, the importance of the triads as a structural construct. In the case of the *itivṛtta*, Bharata is also making his constructs on the number 'five'. There are five constituents of each of the three dimensions of the plot. We may also recall that there were five layers of bricks of the Vedic altar, each representing a different time and spatial order.

The enumeration of the sub-sets of the 'joints' (*sanahıs*) and further divisions are comparable to his analysis of the minor and major joints of the body in the section on *āṅgikābhinaya* (body), and of words, sentences in metre in the context of *vācika* (verbal). In the latter, he had used the word *vṛtta* in metrical patterns.

The two chapters taken together suggest the evolution of a dramatic structure comparable to the body (*śarīra*) with its joints and limbs (*aṅga*) and (*upāṅga*). He makes this explicit at the very beginning of the chapter. However, more important is the modular approach. He provides units and modules and these can be interlocked in an infinite number of ways. Some amongst the *arthaprakṛti* can be omitted; so also the 'joints' (*sandhis*). We must also make the thin but real distinction implied by the two different terms—*sandhi* (both anatomatically and grammatically) and *bandha* (binding, interlacing). In the latter case, the possibilities are even greater for producing new shapes and forms. We will recall the pointed use of this compositional devise in the context of *piṇḍi-bandha* in chapter IV and, later, in Indian poetry and painting, the term is used for a device to produce different geometrical patterns in versification (*chitrabandha*), or in actual figurative art (*narikuñja bandha*) and, of course, *bandha nṛtya*.

Flexibility, challenge of innovation and improvization through a series of combinations, is basic to the abstract design of form devised by Bharata. Indeed, it is *itivṛtta*.

Two statements by Bharata at the end of chapter XXI are clear indication of his approach to all that he has suggested. After describing the characteristics and components of the dramatic form, called *nāṭaka*, he emphasizes the fact that drama presents, re-narrates (*anucaritam*) through *abhinaya* (expression), but its success is possible only when the actor has overcome, suppressed, his personal self (*svabhāvas tajyate*: chapter XXI, v.121–124). Finally, Bharata again stresses that through all that he has suggested, it is possible to present the infinite variety of the world in an innumerable number of forms (*rūpa*). They can be ever new (*navīna*) as also endless (*ananta*). No better statement of a clear vision of intent and flexible structure could be made despite the variant readings and interpretations of these verses.

It was important to underline these principles because they constitute the foundation of the practice of the Indian arts, not only literature and drama. A paradigmatical model with countless possibilities of creating new forms provided an inbuilt flexibility, most visible today in classical Indian music and to an extent, in dance. Ancient and medieval architecture and sculpture, 'drama' and theatre, are structured on these principles.

However, to move on to the next group of chapters, namely, XXII, XXIII, XXIV, XXV and XXVI, we may draw attention only to a few important principles enunciated without going into the details of each of these.

It will be recalled that Bharata had introduced the subject of styles (*vṛttis*), regional schools (*pravṛttis*) and the two modes of presentation (*nāṭya* and *lokadharmī*). He now elaborates upon the *vṛttis* in chapter XXII, goes into the mythical origin of each and the appropriate employment of each, verbal (*bhāratī*), grand (*sāttvatī*), graceful (*kaiśikī*) and energetic (*ārabhaṭī*). Each of the myths of the origin of these styles throws significant light on the nature of predominantly verbal-duel, grand, noble deportment, graceful, lyrical and strong, energetic modes of communication. Bharata sets up a system of correspondence beween these and the expression of the emotive states. We have, as has been pointed out earlier, thus a cluster of principles of *vṛttis, pravṛttis* and *dharmis* along with the controlled and internalized (*ābhyantara*) and external and open (*bāhya*), which corresponds to the emotive states (*sthāyi bhāva*) and *vyabhicāri bhāva* (transient states) on the one hand, and can be employed in all the four instrumentalities of expression, namely, the *abhinayas.* This chapter introduces, in a way, what Bharata elaborates as examples in the subsequent chapters, especially those called *sāmānya* and *citra abhinaya.* Since many, but most of all, V. Raghavan,[13] have expounded on these clusters of principles with masterly command, we restrict ourselves to commenting on the importance of the two chapters on *sāmānya* and *citra abhinaya,* variously translated as general or basic and special or mixed representation.

As regards *sāmānya,* this has to be seen as representing Bharata's concern with the fourth *abhinaya* (i.e. *sāttvika*). He had so far dealt with the body and language (*āṅgika* and *vācika*). After laying out the structure of drama, he takes up the other two, first the outermost *āhārya* (dress, costume, décor, props, masks) and then the innermost *sāttvika.* The chapter on costumes and make-up (XXIII) provides a fund of information on colour, correspondences and understanding of types of make-up for particular characters, people from different parts of India and techniques of constructing stationary and mobile props, including the important banner staff *jarjara* and a vast variety of masks. A series of correspondences are set up. Here also Bharata leaves the door open—'According to one's pleasure, colours can be changed' (XXIII, 97–98).

The chapter on *sāmānya abhinaya* is a long chapter of some fundamental importance. Here, Bharata is endeavouring to state that the 'inner states' of the total personality are fundamental. 'Feeling' and its involuntary expression is his concern. Understandably he emphasizes that *sāmānya abhinaya* relates to all parts of the body—a totality—and not a single gesture which can reflect some feeling which is invisible but can be suggested (XXIII, verses 1,2 and 3: 72 and 73 taken together). Basically, therefore, he is referring to feeling and temperament (*sattva*) which is unexpressed, but it can be discerned through physical signs such as tears, horripilation, etc.

In an earlier chapter (chapter VII, verse 6) Bharata had said that *rasa* (sentiment/mood) arises from the forty-nine types of *bhāva*—eight *sthāyi bhāva*, thirty-three transient states (*vyabhicāri bhāva*) and eight *sāttvika* states when they are imbued with a quality of *sāmānya* (denoting here universality, pervasiveness or commonality). The state proceeding from the thing which is congenial to the heart is the source of *rasa* (sentiment) and it pervades the body just as fire spreads over dry wood (chapter VII, verse 7).

This seminal statement is now elaborated upon in chapter XXIV which he chooses to entitle *sāmānyābhinaya* rather than *sāttvikābhinaya*. The choice of the chapter heading is significant. Bharata's purpose is to draw attention to universality and pervasiveness. Its source is *manas* (mind).

Although scholars have commented on the chapter on *sāmānyābhinaya*, it has perhaps not been examined closely for identifying some fundamentals of the senses—body, mind relationship Bharata introduces in the chapter. We have drawn attention to the importance given to the senses, organs and perceptions in speculative thought (the Upaniṣads and Bharata's statement on theatre as the world of the eye and ear, the visible and the audible). In this chapter, he takes up the fundamental issue of the relationship of the senses and the mind, psychic states and involuntary reflection or recognizable signs of inner depression and elation through physical reflexes.

Bharata pays attention to all the five senses, presents his classification and categories of 'personality types' and different types of human temperament. Tacitly, he is following in the latter, the classification of personality types of the Ayurvedic system where individuals have different types of temperament, calm, cool, hot, excitable, energetic or dull, depending upon their metabolism caused by the relative balance or imbalance of the primary elements of *vāta, pitta, kapha,* etc.

Looked at thus, the chapter reveals Bharata's keen observant eye and mental comprehension of the senses—body, mind, feeling, emotion, relationship. Personality types of individuals, mannerisms of particular types in walk, gait, carriage, body-language and speech of the young and the old, men and women, are indicators of this relationship. Bharata points out: 'a person out of his mind (*mana*) cannot know the objects of senses which come through the five sources' (XXIV, 86). Obviously, Bharata is alluding to the presence or absence of 'consciousness' (*cetanā*) and experience. He makes a clear distinction between mind (*manas*), *bhāva* (feeling) and sense perceptions.

Although at the explicit level, Bharata appears only to be giving instructions on how to represent the sense of sound (*śābda*), touch (*sparśa*), form (*rūpa*) and smell (*gandha*) and taste (*rasa*), he is, in fact, drawing attention to a deeper aspect of the senses, body, mind, feeling, relationship. This is evident from the verses which follow (XXIV, verses 86 to 96).

It is at this stage that he places *kāma* (understood as both desire and love) at the centre of his concern. Sense perceptions, feeling and consciousness are the basis of the man-woman relationship. Bharata pinpoints both. There is desire for wealth (*artha-kāma*), desire for virtue, duty (*dharma-kāma*), and even desire for *mokṣa* (*mokṣa-kāma*) and there is the whole world of desire for desire in the man-woman relationship. Stated pithily and without much ado, these are perceptions of a fundamental universal nature which would cross all culture-specific boundaries. Bharata's insights into the nature of human consciousness, the working of the mind, feeling, body and sense in concord are, nevertheless, only explicitly stated as identification of personality types and classification and categories of men and women, largely women here, and the outward signs of recognizing character or personality traits. The general context is the sphere of *kāma* (desire and love) and, therefore, intra-gender communication. The nature and levels of communication are introvert and extrovert, inner or outer. Pertinently, it is in this context that he describes the different types of graces (*alaṁkāra*) or women, namely, feeling (*bhāva*), emotion (*hāva*) and passion (*helā*). These are not autonomous categories: they are psychic states with their emotional and involuntary reflex physical response co-ordinates in relation to the opposite sex (XXIV, verses 6–11) and in the sphere of *kāma* (normally, most inadequately translated as *erotic*). The underlying foundation of the entire chapter is thus *kāma* and senses, body, mind and consciousness relationship. Logically, at the level of perception and expression, these are either inner or outer (*ābhyantara* and *bāhya*) or indirect, implicit or invisible (*parokṣa*) and direct and explicit (*pratyakṣa*). Another group of terms, namely, *sūcī* (pointing needle), *aṅkura* (sprouting), *śākhā* (branches) indicate the feeling, body and word-gesture relationship in different sequential order or concurrency, suggestive or proliferated. It is on these foundations of perception and insight, that Bharata narrows down his concern from the generic character and personality types of women to the categories of heroines (*nāyikā*). Understandably, the classification of the *nāyikās* has dominated Indian artistic history and continues to do so in the performing arts. However, it would be worthwhile to remember the context in which Bharata enumerates this classification of the heroine-types.

This is even more evident when we look at the next

chapter which *prima facie* deals with courtesans, but is, in fact, concerned with men, types of men and types of heroes. Bharata juxtaposes the two genders and considers the response of one sex in relation to the other, but all in the sphere of *kāmatantra* (XXV, 53–54). The classifications are impressive. We may also find them somewhat amusing, even archaic, because the nature of human relationships even between men and women in the spheres of love and desire is far more complex and uncategorizable. Nevertheless, there are some brilliant insights into relationships and typologies which could emerge in this sphere. More important is his identification of the nature of consciousness, mind and feeling and its outer manifestation through 'carriage', gait, facial muscle contraction and relaxation, tension and release. Normally, all this is not, as we know, reflected only in one part of the body; it is pervasive and it permeates all aspects which we easily recognize as personal style.

In these chapters, there are other concepts and terms which assume the dimensions of highly technical terms in later writing on the arts, such as, *pratyakṣa* (explicit) and *parokṣa* (implicit), *ābhyantara* (inner) and *bāhya* (outer). Two other terms are *natiyita* and *nivṛtyaṅkura* (XXIV, 41–46). Bharata also reminds us of the importance of *dhruvā* songs. He, however, explicates these only later.

But it is time now to make a few brief comments on chapter XXVI which concludes all matters of concept, structure and design, namely, *Citrābhinaya* (translated, special enactment, special representation, mixed pictorial, a category of different types of enacting through speech and movement). There has been some discussion on the fine line of distinction between *sāmānyābhinaya* and *citrābhinaya.* There has been also a near unanimity on the conclusion that there is some confusion or lack of clarity and, certainly, ambiguity. Seen again in the light of our observations on Bharata's concern with personality, temperament and inner states of consciousness, especially in human relationships, in the chapter on *sāmānyābhinaya* the chapter on *citrābhinaya* is distinct and different. The emphasis moves from person to objects and phenomena. Appropriately, the chapter restricts itself to describing methods and manner of representing objects at different distances and heights, naturally, including birds, animals and human beings (when swooning or angry, etc.), numbers and all dimensions of time—past, present and future, and finally, the cycle of daily, annual time and the seasons. Bharata's intent is clear. *Citrābhinaya* as a category can be clearly distinguished from *sāmānyābhinaya.* Three general statements made here are of importance because they throw light on the earlier discussion on the interconnection of *bhāva, vibhāva* and *anubhāva* and how *citrābhinaya* is the support system of *anubhāva* (consequents). The states (*bhāva*) relate to the feeling of one's own self and determinants (*vibhāva*) is the process of communication, literally exhibition (*pradarśana*) to the other. *Anubhāva* (consequents) is all else, that is outwardly. Naturally, *citrābhinaya* is the proper tool of creating the atmosphere. Of significance are the last ten verses of the chapter. Bharata sums up in a nutshell all that he has outlined in the preceding chapters. Since they have been overlooked, by and large, an excerpt of verses 115 to 129 in full would not be out of place. In the fifteen verses (XXVI, 115–129) Bharata sums up all that he has tried to enunciate at the level of goal, concept, manifestation, visualization, structure and technique:

"115–116. Just as the garland-maker makes garlands

from various kinds of flowers, the drama should be produced similarly by gestures and different limbs, and by sentiments and states.

116–117 Movements and gaits that have been prescribed by the rules for a character who has entered the stage, should be maintained by the actor without giving up the (particular) temperament till he makes an exit.

117–118. Now, I have finished speaking about the representation to be made through words and gestures. Things omitted here by me should be gathered from (the usage of) the people (*loka-vyavahara*).

The triple basis of drama:

118–119. The people (*loka*), the Vedas and the spiritual faculty (*adhyatma*) are known as the three authorities. The drama is mostly based on objects related to the last two (the Vedas and the *adhyātma*).

119–120. The drama which has its origin in the Vedas, and the spiritual faculty (*adhyātma*) and includes proper words and metre, succeeds (*siddham*) when it is approved of by the people (*loka*). Hence, the people are considered as the (ultimate) authority (*pramāna*) on the drama.

121. A mimicry (*anukarana*) (literally a re-narration, a re-statement of a presentation and not imitation) of the exploits of gods, sages, kings, as well as of householders in this world, is called the drama. (Literally, presentation of that which has been: *purvavrta carita*)

122. When human character with all its different states is represented with (suitable) gestures it is called the drama.

People supplying norm to the drama:

123. Thus, the events (*vārtā*) relating to the people in all their different conditions, may be (literally, should be) included in a play, by those well versed in the canons of drama (*natyaveda*) (also *nāṭyavidhāna*).

124. Whatever *sastras*, laws, arts and activities are connected with the human conduct (*lokadharma*) may be produced (literally called) as a drama.

125. Rules regarding the feelings and activities of the world, moveable as well as immovable, cannot be formulated (literally ascertained) exhaustively by the *śāstra.*

126. The people have different dispositions, and on their dispositions the drama rests. Hence, playwrights and producers (*prayoktṛ*) should take the people as their authority (as regards the rules of the art).

127. Thus, they (*prayoktṛ*) should pay attention to the feelings, gestures and the temperament in representing the states of various characters (that may appear in the drama).

128. The men who know in this order the art of histrionic representation and apply it on the stage, receive in this world the highest honour for putting into practice the theory or essence of drama (*naṭyatattva*) as well as (the art of) acting (*abhinaya*).

129. These are to be known as the modes of representation dependent on words, costumes, make-up and gestures. An expert in dramatic production (*prayoga*) should adopt these for the success (in his undertaking)."

The verses, with the Sanskrit originals of some terms in this welcome and yet inadequate translation by M.M. Ghosh, almost speak for themselves.

The sphere and levels, approach, method and humility is unambiguous.

We may only underscore once again the use of the terms *nāṭyaveda* and *nāṭyatattva, adhyātma* and *loka.* He has, indeed, created a wide world of flexibility with scope for creativity and innovation. It is a unified single vision manifested in multiple forms. He does synthesize the world of essence, the world of reflection (*nāṭyaveda* and *nāṭya-*

tattva) and feeling, with that of structure and grammar (*vidhāna* and *śāstra*). The ultimate judges are the people (*loka*).[14] They can accept, reject, change or modify. Earlier, he had told us that he may have left out much and for this *loka-vyavahāra* is to be observed. Thus, universality and specificity, abstraction and generalization, the structured and flexible, are interpenetrating levels. From the point of view of a clear statement, chapter XXVI and these verses are another 'pause' or watershed of the *Nāṭyaśāstra.*

Having laid out in a nutshell his concept and design, Bharata now turns his attention to the 'final product'—the theatrical spectacle as a whole. The acid test of any creativity, from inspiration to the process of transference of 'idea' to 'form', from the abstract to the 'concrete', is the 'product', complete and 'autonomous', which must communicate at varying levels to different audiences—culture specific and trans-cultural contexts. While being in defined finite time and place, it must have power to communicate beyond time and place.

It is these sets of issues to which Bharata draws attention in chapter XXVII. He is clear that the efficacy of the artist's creation (*siddhi*—translated as 'success', denoting also command and empowerment from achievement) lies in its ability to communicate. Bharata identifies two levels—the divine (*daivika*) and the human (*mānuṣī*). We must understand these terms to denote the different levels of consciousness. In our language we may even interpret them as intuitive, inspirational, acausal and discursive, supramental and mundane, gross or subtle, but not 'sacred' and 'profane': (chapter XXVII, 1–2). An artistic creation, a theatre production, can uplift, elevate the spectator to a sense of awe, wonder (*adbhuta*) and complete 'silence' as response (Chapter XXVII, 17), and thus evoke speechless reverberation, or it can communicate to evoke response at lesser degrees of refinement and at more explicit levels of applause through words *sādhu sādhu* or clapping.

The creator artist, dramatist and actor, can achieve this only through inner control and discipline. It is in this context that the word *sādhaka* is used (chapter XXVII, 86). Bharata reminds us that the entire act of creation and presentation is a *sādhanā* where impersonalization, depersonalization and detachment is primary.

As for the audience and spectators, they too must be attuned, trained and initiated. The demand from them is no less exacting. Preparedness both of attitude and initiation into some technicalities is an essential pre-requisite. They are also potential artists: the artistic creation re-stimulates and energizes dormant states. It is these verses on the audience (*prekṣaka*) which stimulated an active debate for centuries on the nature of aesthetic response.

Bharata does not forget critics and judges and lays down the qualification of a jury. The list is daunting. It must comprise of an expert in ritual (*yajñavit*), a dancer (*nartaka*), a prosodist (*chandovit*), a grammarian (*śabdavit*), a king (*rājan*), an expert in archery (*iṣvastravit*), painter (*citravit*), courtesan (*veśyā*), musician (*gandharva*) and a king's officer (*rājasevaka*). Could we wish for a more comprehensive list of discipline areas to be represented as adjudicators? Perhaps, Bharata should have added a medical man (*yoga* specialist) and an architect.

The next few chapters deal with the broad spectrum of music. Bharata is concerned with the formal aspects of all categories of music, instrumental and vocal (chapters XXVIII to XXXIII). Here, he outlines his system and lays down the formal principles (*vidhāna* and *vidhi* are the two words used). We will recall that he had introduced the subject of voice production 'notes' (*svaras*) in the context of prosody. Now, he picks it up for elaboration. These chapters lay the foundations of a distinctive system of music—its micro-intervals (*śruti*), notes (*svara*), scales (*grāma*), modes (*mūrcchanā*), melodic forms (*jātis*), rhythm (*tāḷa*) and much else. The classifications follow the same pattern of 'levels' and 'dimensions'. He breaks up the whole to its smallest constituents and then develops an architectonic structure. There is so much of 'value' in these chapters, that no justice can be done even to the rich contents and vocabulary of these chapters in the present work. Bharata displays an extraordinary knowledge of material in the making of musical instruments (four types) and of the nature of sound, notes, consonance, assonance, dissonance and melodic forms. He establishes a system of correspondence between each category and its potential for arousing emotion; he develops it to establish patterns of configuration of 'notes' in melodic forms and emotive states. He distinguishes between vocal and instrumental music. He further divides vocal music into two types—one, consisting only of notes and the other, with words (*varṇa* and *geya*). He provides details of different types of instruments and their respective characteristics. He returns to an elaboration of the category of *dhruvā* songs which he had mentioned in many earlier chapters. He identifies a category of music called *gāndharva* and distinguishes it from *gāna*. Bharata enumerates the different types of *tāla* (time measures—rhythm, metrical cycles). In short, he lays down the foundation of a distinctly Indian style of music with its scales and modal structure. This was debated and discussed, even modified and changed, but the underlying principles were never rejected. Bharata, as in the case of *āṅgika* (body language) *vācika* (verbal expression) and in respect of plot (*itivṛtta*), provides a basic framework with several components which can be used as 'modules' in an infinite number of configurations to produce multiple and subsidiary forms. It is this inbuilt flexibility which has facilitated the twin phenomena of unbroken continuity at one level, and constant movement or change and flux, at the other. The history of Indian classical music in theory and practice is the most convincing and vibrant example.

The chapters are full of general principles and methodologies (*vidhāna* and *vidhi*), not *niyama* (rules), as also technicalities. They constitute a fountainhead for discussion on music and the several streams that flowed out of the *Nāṭyaśāstra* for centuries. There has been a rich and interesting discussion on these subjects, at the 'conceptual' as also technical levels. We may only draw attention to his elaboration of the form called *lāsya* which he had alluded to in an earlier chapter.

Normally, in contemporary usage the term has been used in opposition to the term *tāṇḍava* in the field of dance. Bharata does not establish these as a pair. For Bharata this is a form of solo-composition where one actor performs different roles without change of costume to the accompaniment of music, vocal or instrumental. The actor or dancer can sit, stand or move while performing. The context is generally in relation to women performers. In elaborating upon this category in the chapters on music and presenting sub-categories, Bharata underpins the fundamental and crucial role of music and *tāla* in all that we understand by the generic term *abhinaya* in the repertoire of contemporary classical dance.

The discussion on *dhruvā* songs is important because many technical details of the *pūrvaraṅga* cannot be comprehended without their explanation in these chapters.

There can be little doubt about the integrity of the text, conceived as a whole but the relative incorrectness and corruptness of the text can certainly be doubted.

As in the case of the styles (*vṛttis*) and regional schools (*pravṛttis*) and modes (*dharmis*), there is a body of valuable and critical literature by modern scholars ranging from Swami Prajnanananda to Premlata Sharma[15] and it is neither possible nor perhaps necessary to analyse further.

The last three chapters (XXXIV to XXXVI) conclude this mighty text. Chapters XXXIV and XXXV are concerned with another group of issues. Chapter XXXV brings us back to the beginning. While Bharata had spoken of types of characters as also heroes and heroines earlier, here he elaborates upon them in more specific terms and also relates them to the practical problem of casting of roles in a theatrical production. His guidelines in most cases would still be applicable although the number of character types, heroes and anti-heroes may have to be greatly enlarged to include the proliferation of disciplines and specialists as also new socio-economic phenomena. Had Bharata lived today he may have laid down guidelines for casting not only the roles of kings, queens, attendants, military personnel, jesters, but would have included politicians, high-ranking professionals, businessmen, academicians, scientists, technocrats, brokers and innumerable others, in their identifiable and recognizable lifestyles and consequent vocabulary, body-language, intonation and attire. We are familiar with the widespread employment of stock-characters in Indian drama and on the screen. Bharata is a distant antecedent of these trends, not all totally aesthetically satisfying.

Instead, of greater importance are the other organizational matters relating to the drama group (theatre company in our language) He lays down the qualifications and equipment of all members of the troupe. The list is exhaustive. It includes anyone from the poet (*kavi*) to the dramatist and script-writer (*nāṭyakāra*), the director (*sūtra-dhāra*), the actor-dancer (*naṭa*), the actress (*nāṭakīyā*), a jester (*vidūṣaka*), a master-musician (*tauripa*), an expert in orchestration (*kuśīlava*), a costume designer (*veṣakāra*), a head-gear expert (*mukuṭa-kāraka* or *śīrṣaka*), maker of ornaments (*ābharaṇakṛt*), a maker of garlands (*mālyakṛt*), a theatre designer and carpenter (*kāru*), a painter (*citra-kāra*), a dyer (*rajaka*) and other professional 'artists' and craftsmen. All these constitute the company, called by the generic term *bharatas*. This list could profitably match the credit-list of any theatrical performance, other than those who provide sound and light effects.

Bharata's command over the whole range of creativity from the source of creation, inspiration of the artist, to the artistic process and expression through the principal instrumentalities of expression of the verbal and corporeal to the final product, communication and response, is overwhelming. His knowledge and competence of practical details and consciousness of team-work are impressive. He has, indeed, created a *śāstra* of *prayoga*, a framework of principles of 'praxis' or practice.

Significantly and purposefully, he changes the level of his discourse in the concluding chapter. We return to the beginning, not to an identical moment of the origin of drama in the state of meditation and reflection of Brahma's *samādhi*, but to the few but important queries of the assembly of sages who heard Bharata's exposition. The names include Ātreya, Vasiṣṭha, Aṅgiras, Agastya, Manu, Viśvāmitra, Jamadagni, Mārkaṇḍeya, Bharadvāja, Vālmīki, Kaṇva and many others. They are all creators of many branches of knowledge.

Their questions revolve around three issues: the

significance of the elaborate preliminaries (*purvaraṅga*), why does the director (*sūtradhāra*) perform the rites of ablution (and *pūja*) on stage and how did drama come down (literally, drop down) to earth and how did the actors (descendants of Bharata) come to be equated with the fourth caste, the Śūdras?

Bharata's replies are significant. They are cogent at the level of structure but more at the level of meaning. The preliminaries are like an armour. Just as the body has an armour to protect, the preliminaries provide the initial armour of maintaining and sustaining the world of the 'imagination' (*anukīrtana,* a new creation of the universal, that which can happen and be communicated) in the body (*śarīra*) of drama. It heralds auspiciousness (*maṅgala*). To this day we know the significance of formal auspicious beginnings and inaugurals in all facets of Indian life. Thus, the preliminaries (*pūrvaraṅga*) have the dual role of protection and of heralding. Its significance in linking the different levels of the divine (*daivika*) and the human (*mānuṣī*), of the celestial and terrestrial, we have already drawn attention to. Through the device of repeated entrances and exits of a group of three men in different guises, each time a different spatial and temporal order is represented and interlinked.

Bharata goes further here and equates the sound of the *nāndi* to the exposition of the Vedic *mantras,* the music to a holy bath and repetitive recitation (*japa*).

To the second question, why the (director) *sūtradhāra* performs ablutions, Bharata, at the explicit level, gives a practical answer. The pouring of water becomes necessary because by now he (i.e. the *sūtradhāra*) has bent so many times, he requires relief. At the implicit level, Bharata is drawing attention to the transition from one level of communication to another. The sacralization of space and time over, a pausation is necessary. From this moment, the director (*sūtradhāra*) recedes to the background and the drama proper appears.

The answer to the third question, as we have pointed out before (story of the descent of drama to the earth and the curse), is a pointer towards the primary and fundamental requirement of the eschewing of personal 'ego' and pride of the artist.

The twin demands for 'impersonality' and 'intensity' and authenticity, and of negative capability and sensitivity are stressed. Internal discipline and concentration (*tapas*) is of essence. This is the message of the curse on Urvaśī to descend to earth when she said 'Purūravas' instead of 'Purushottama' in a performance at Indra's court.

Bharata's sons (the creative community) also have to go through a series of expiation acts (*prāyaścitta*) because of 'ego' or misuse of their powers, before they are once again rehabilitated on earth through the intervention of King Nahuṣa

With extraordinary finesse and skill, Bharata brings his exposition to a culmination by restating the totality of the original inspiration, the process of transference from the unified undifferentiated state to expression through concrete form and multiple forms, the dimensions and levels of communication and the demands of depersonalization, humility, training and discipline of the artist. But all said and done, the creative act is a mystery and there are many aspects which are secret. *Guha* is the repeated word (chapter XXVI, 9, 10, 11, etc).

The sequential narration of the thirty-six chapters was necessary to reveal the structure of the text at its implicit and explicit levels. There is a unified vision, a well-defined integral structure and a methodology of discourse, which moves on many levels and through different circuits, and is multidisciplinary in nature. His organizational pattern is also circular like his notion of plot (*itivṛtta*). There is, no doubt, possibility of interpolation (the most outstanding and difficult example is that of the section on *śānta rasa*) and corrupt readings but the steel frame of his exposition has a unique integrity of vision.

To briefly sum up, the sequential movement of the text is along the circumference of a circle with an unseen but real centre and point. Chapters I, II, III, IV and V are one group, where spatial and temporal relations are outlined. Chapters VI and VII are a second group, where life is abstracted into a spectrum of *rasa, bhāva* and their variations. Chapters VIII, IX, X, XI, XII and XIII deal with all aspects of body-language. Chapter XIII comes as a pause to concretize the methodology of transforming space to place on the stage. Chapters XIV, XV, XVI, XVII, XVIII and XIX deal with all aspects of the verbal, sound and speech (*vācika*). Another major pausation occurs with chapters XX and XXI which deal with the structure of drama, types of plays and the multilayered movement of the plot. *Time* is the concern. Chapters XXII, XXIII, XXIV and XXV and XXVI constitute another group which deals with matters which relate to the other two instrumentalities of expression, costuming and décor (XXIII) and *sāttvika* (XXIV). Matters which are of a general nature are considered in chapter XXII, on styles (*vṛttis*), pervasive matters in the second half of chapter XXIV, on *sāmānyābhinaya* and *citrābhinaya* (mixed or pictorial, XXVI) and gender-relationships (XXVII). There is another pause to consider dramatic success and achievements. Chapters XXVIII, XXIX, XXX, XXXI, XXXII and XXXIII are devoted to music. These are followed by two chapters on distribution of roles and organization (XXXIV and XXXVI), and in chapter XXXVI the circle is completed by returning to the origin of drama and its descent from the heavens.

It will be observed that Bharata devotes equal attention to each of the principal tools, namely, body-language (*āṅgika*), words and language (*vācika*) and music (vocal and instrumental). The structural and formal aspects of each are analysed. Structural matters, he takes up in the pausation chapters of *kakṣāvibhāga* (zonal divisions), plot and pervasive general matters in another group, followed by another pause on dramatic success and response. Organizational matters constitute a separate group.

This grand design, Bharata executes as a master conceiver of a great orchestra. He assigns a role to each instrument, lays down the plan of each group of instruments, their interaction with each other, the phasing and the movement, never forgetting that all this is for the evocation of a 'mood', a state, where once each instrument and player has played a part, they are no longer important and meaningful. Like the actors of his drama, the *āṅgika*, the *vācika*, the *āhārya* and *sāttvika* must transcend their individual identity and merge in the totality. Just as the instruments of an orchestra have their distinctive identity and special techniques of playing, each *abhinaya* (extended to art) is distinct and clearly identifiable, has a role to play in the totality, but is never absolutely autonomous.

While in the matter of organization of his work the comparison with an orchestra for playing a great symphony is pertinent, in the matter of the movement of consideration of issues and levels of discourse, the text is more like a piece of Indian music. It begins in a mood of reflection, unfolds the entire gamut of sounds, moves through permutations, combinations, and returns, as it were, to the tonic of the melodic system or the first beat of the Indian *tāla* system, namely, *sama*.

Also, we have stressed the eclectic character of the undertaking and the synthesizing role of the *Natyasastra.* It is a confluence of many streams of thought, life, conduct, the arts. For a while, it becomes a big lake, almost oceanic in proportion. Naturally, from this 'confluence', lake or mini-ocean, many different streams were to flow out.

Bharata provided the basic framework and a pan-Indian vocabulary which was to guide the theory and practice of the Indian arts for two millennia. The course of the flow had twin dynamics; one of a life-line of perennial immutability and continuity, and the other of change and flux.

NOTES AND REFERENCES

1 Kapila Vatsyayan, *The Square and the Circle of the Indian Arts,* Roli Books International, New Delhi, 1983, pp. 23–27.

2 H.N. Chakravarti, '*Bīja*', in *Kalātattvakośa: A Lexicon of Fundamental Concepts of the Indian Arts,* Vol. I, edited by Bettina Bäumer, General Editor: Kapila Vatsyayan, Indira Gandhi National Centre for the Arts and Motilal Banarsidass, Delhi, 1988, pp. 117–33.

3. '*Puruṣa'*, ibid., pp. 23–40; Kapila Vatsyayan, *The Square and the Circle of the Indian Arts,* pp. 27–29; Stella Kramrisch, 'The Temple as Purusa', *Studies in Indian Temple Architecture,* edited by Pramod Chandra, American Institute of Indian Studies, Varanasi, 1975, pp. 40–47.

4. Kapila Vatsyayan, 'Indian Art—One and the Many', Nehru Memorial Lecture, 1993 (under publication).

5. F.B.J. Kuiper, *Varuṇa and Vidūṣaka: On the Origin of Sanskrit Drama,* North Holland, Amsterdam, 1979, p. 153. Kuiper holds this view on account of a different list of deities in chapters I, II and III. He is of the view that these, along with some others, are the work of a devout Saivite.

6. F.B.J. Kuiper, ibid. See the comprehensive discussion on the '*jarjara*', pp. 119–153, etc. Kuiper brilliantly sums up the nineteenth and twentieth century discussion on the '*jarjara.*'. His footnotes are particularly illuminating.

7. Kapila Vatsyayan, *The Square and the Circle of the Indian Arts,* pp. 60–65, for analysis of different phases; F.B.J. Kuiper, *Varuna and*

Vidūṣaka: On the Origin of Sanskrit Drama, pp.166–174; Natalia Lidova, *Drama and Ritual of Early Hinduism,* Motilal Banarsidass, Delhi, 1994, pp. 7–24.

8. Kapila Vatsyayan, *Classical Indian Dance in Literature and the Arts,* Sangeet Natak Akademi, New Delhi, 2nd edn., 1977, pp. 38–97.
9. K.D. Tripathi, '*Lakṣaṇa*', in *Kalātattvakośa,* Vol. I, pp. 135–45.
10. M.C. Byrsky, *Concepts of Ancient Indian Theatre,* Munshiram Manoharlal, Delhi, 1994, pp. 101–44; also see Abhinavagupta's extensive commentary on *Nātyasastra,* Vol. III, Baroda edition.
11. Kapila Vatsyayan, *The Square and the Circle of the Indian Arts,* on *Itivṛtta.*, pp. 47–48.
12. Sāgaranandin, *Nāṭakalakṣaṇaratnakośa,* edited by Myles Dillon, American Philosophical Society, 1937; also see 'Introduction' by V. Raghavan in revised edition, 1960. Also, see full discussion on *itivṛtta* in *Nāṭakalakṣaṇaratnakośa* text edited by Balram Shankar, Chowkhamba Sanskrit series, Varanasi, 1972, pp. 7–104. It is a very full and comprehensive discussion.
13. V. Raghavan, *Sanskrit Drama, Its Aesthetics and Production,* 1993 chapters on '*Vṛttis*', pp. 242–315 and '*Naṭya and Lokadharmī*', pp 201–242. Also see Kapila Vatsyayan, 'Margī and Deśī' and 'Naṭya and Lokadharmi', *Sternbach Memorial Lecture,* Vol. I, Bhāratīya Sanskrit Pariṣad, Lucknow, 1979.
14. V.N. Misra and P.L. Sharma, '*Loka*' in *Kalātattvakośa,* Vol. II, pp. 119–196. The word '*Loka*' has a pervasive meaning. It is a fundamental concept. Bharata's use of the term is contextually loaded.
15. Prajnanananda, Swami, *A History of Indian Music,* Vol. I, Ramakrishna Vedanta Math, Calcutta, 1963; Premlata Sharma, *Saharasa,* Sangeet Natak Akademi; Mukund Lath, *Dattilam,* Introduction, Impex India, New Delhi, 1978; Alain Danielou, *Introduction to the Study of Musical Scales,* pp. 1–11, where concepts are defined.

5

The Text and Creativity

While the rather long sequential narration of the *Nāṭya-sastra* may have taxed the patience of readers, it was necessary. Often, all too often, the text has been broken up into fragments and each interpreter or group of specialists have looked at it either only as their text, or a text which addresses itself only to highly abstruse issues or technical details. This analysis may have also made clear the special characteristics of a *śāstra* as a category in the Indian tradition. It is neither theory nor praxis, nor purely speculative or empirical. It has a definite purpose (*uddesa*) and a clear structure. It is a well-defined critical discourse and can be couched in a language of 'myth' so that the multiple layers of discourse can be sustained.

Once the *Nāṭyaśāstra* was created, it influenced both the critical discourse as also creativity, not only in the theatre arts, literature, poetry, music and dance, but also in architecture, sculpture and painting.

While it is not the purpose of this monograph to go into the sphere of the applicability of the theory to actual artistic creations from Bhasa and Kālidāsa's plays to contemporary traditional Indian theatre, or music—Hindustani, Carnatic, the styles of dance, the many schools and styles of architecture, sculpture and music, it would perhaps be pertinent to restate in general and not in technical terms, how the world-view, the theoretical principles enunciated by Bharata, especially the goal of artistic creation as a tool to evoke a *rasa* (aesthetic relish, *āsvāda*) and not to look at or imitate actuality, is manifested in the different arts. While both the inspiration and the final goal are similar, if not identical, the formal aspects and techniques are different.

These underlying principles provide a fundamental unity of vision to the Indian arts, extendable to the South-east Asian arts, while leaving immense scope for regional identities, individual styles, and an infinite number of variations and modifications.

Until the eighteenth, in some cases, the nineteenth century, this was true of all the arts, with varying degrees of sophistication and excellence. Thereafter is a break and another phase of the modern sensibility emerges, especially in literature, architecture, sculpture and painting. We are confining our remarks to the general applicability of Bharata's perceptions to the early and medieval phases of Indian art.

So, what is the Indian artist's concern and how does it express itself through the particular medium?

The search for 'totality' and 'wholeness': totality (*pūrṇa* and *akhaṇḍa*) and trans-personal is primary. The nascent stage is unmanifested but intensely experienced. It expresses itself through a multiplicity of forms, all abstract and universalized, non-contextualized, so to say. The 'forms' with their typologies of the mythic and the human world recreate, replicate, re-narrate, re-state, re-model the 'incipient' experience of *bhāva*. This is *anukīrtana, anukathana, anukṛṣṭi, anucarita.* It is manifestation of states of being with both a sense of distance as also intensity. Eschewing of the particular 'I' is a primary demand. It is not imitation or mirroring of actuality or imitation of a single 'ideal' or an absolute. This re-recreation is a mini-micro or a macro form, in a small shrine or a great temple, diminutive sculptor or monumental sculpture, mural or miniature, a full drama or a lyric, a full theatrical spectacle or a solo performance, an orchestra or a solo performance which becomes a 'prism' for seeing and hearing many colours—all only to suggest or evoke a single 'unified' luminosity. This is the singular *rasa* of the beginning and the end: all else is play (*līlā, krīḍā*) of forms in specific configurations serving a very important and indispensable, but nevertheless ephemeral function. Heightened and charged experience is the source and the ultimate goal. If achieved, the artistic 'product' is empowered in contexts specific and defined, and communicates beyond context in 'space' and 'time'. If not, the artistic product is skilful (*kuśala*), dexterous but never uplifting or inspiring.

Bharata provided a vast vocabulary of formal elements of each mode of expression, so did the *śāstras* of architecture, sculpture, painting, music and dance. These were so useful and challenging as games that often the artistic creation was the configuration of all the formal elements (the *śarīra,* body of drama, the *itivṛtta* of Bharata) but without soul (*ātman*). This was and continues to be an inherent challenge of the Indian traditional arts. Since the demand of the 'sacrifice' of the individuated subjective-self is great, it requires a 'life of discipline'. This alone may facilitate the inner happening of the invisible heightened experience. This is the 'unsaid' invisible 'seed' (*bīja*) of creativity. However, this may or may not happen, and yet the tools available for a formal language of the arts are so chiselled that it can happen that the artistic product remains at the level of deadly correctness of formal elements, skilful and competent, but is not energized with life-breath (*prāṇa*) from within. This is as true of good and bad poetry, inspired or only correct, as of monumental architecture, sculpture, paintings, music and dance. When the intuitive heightened experience permeates the structure like fire ignites wood, or all the elements become a continuous ring of fire (*alātacakra*), the artistic creation uplifts, elevates and liberates. If not, it is repetitive in theme, content and structure. There are countless examples of both in the panorama of the Indian arts. There are thousands of Naṭarāja images, many correct, only a handful charged. The same composition of a *varṇa* is correctly performed by dancers. Only a few, even that only on particular occasions, evoke a sense of transcendence. Indian music in performance is the most obvious example.

However, all the arts, at their best, in the past or present, can be comprehended through the world-view outlined and Bharata's principles of 'structure'. Since we cannot go into the history of creativity in all the arts and the specific applicability of Bharata's theory, we shall attempt to state this in general terms for general readers.

Indian architecture, whether the *stūpas* or the temples or the city-plans or domestic architecture, is created on the concept of *bīja* (seed), *bindu* (point) and *puruṣa.* The mud-walls, the brick and stone, ground or elevation plans are an orchestration of multiple forms flowing out of and flowing into a centre. Invariably, it begins with a point of unity and manifests itself through a spectrum of multiple forms which, in turn, evoke harmony and equanimity. There is, first and foremost, a centre. The centre enlarges itself into a vast complex either as a circle or as a square, is filled with crowded abundance of life in all its variety. The ornamentation and the decoration, representational or abstract, play their role to an ascending oneness vertically, and a closing in and gathering of all energies horizontally from the outer to the inner. Brick by brick, stone by stone, an immense epic poem of the infinite is made. Each detail can be separated, but in fact, none is autonomous; each unit is a part of the whole, interwoven and interlocked. In its totality, it represents heaven on earth, the central mountain, the Sumeru. Ultimately, it is the cosmic order on earth arousing the dominant mood of wonder (*vismaya*) and evoking a transcendental experience of bliss, whether the observer, participator or pilgrim moves from the outside to the inside, or circumbulates the *stūpa* or temple until he reaches the centre which represents the ultimate void, the *śūnya*, *nirvāṇa* or *mokṣa.* Alternately, he figuratively ascends the pinnacle, whether in the austere simplicity of the spherical dome of the *stūpa*, or through the crowded multiplicity of the temple. Sanchi and Bharhut, the temples of northern, southern, western or eastern India, speak the same language of transcendence and of heightened experience despite the cultural specifics of each of these monuments. Impersonality and intensity are the twin paradoxical demands of this art which is life-bound and goes beyond it. These monuments bear testimony to the concretization of this vision through a perfect language of art, which was as pan-Indian as specific in time, region or locality.

Sculpture, likewise, manifests this vision of wholeness through a methodology of impersonalization. Indian figurative art is not portraiture of the specific. Each image is an embodiment of a dominant abstracted impersonalized state or mood in a given stance or pose, evoking stillness and dynamic movement together. Each is a complete world unto itself, related to life, born of life, part of the cultural fabric, but not it. Buddha is the Buddha, the historical prince Siddhārtha and Śākyamuni, but he is more: he is compassion, pathos and grace in absolute. The spirit and soul of the cosmic infinite is contained in the body of the particular but impersonal form. The image is not the historical figure—it is and it is not the culture-specific in which it is articulated: a Kuṣāṇa, Gupta, Pāla, or for that matter, an Indonesian, a Khmer, Japanese and Chinese Buddha are clearly identifiable. They are distinguishable and dateable, but in the last analysis, they are beyond their cultural boundaries and are each a hypothesis, an aspect of the vast ocean of *karuṇā* (compassion) in all its multitudes of shades, tones and subtleties. The dominant mood of compassion (*karuṇā*) is encircled sometimes with many transient states, represented as the vegetation, flora, fauna, *yakṣīs,* dryads, *gandharvas* and *apsaras,* each playing a specific role in building the totality, or it may be the single austere simple statement of the still centre of peace and enlightenment, suggested through the symbols of the Buddha, the Bodhi tree, sandals, etc., or the human figure. Some contain the variety and some eschew it, but the impersonalized intensity of the mood of compassion is the residual taste, everlasting and universal.

The images of Śiva and Viṣṇu in their benign or demonic moods, as *yogīs* or *sadāśivas,* as lovers or ascetics containing bi-unity as androgynes (*Ardhanārīśvara*) or combining the three principles of involution, evolution and devolution, as conjoined images of Brahmā, Viṣṇu and Maheśa or only the principle of creation and destruction as Harihara, or as four-faced or three-faced *liṅgas,* all articulate, once again, the same attribute of the internalized intangible experience of the unmanifested unity. The multiple faces and arms of the image are parts of the whole and vehicles for the final evocation of the transcendental experience of bliss (*rasa*). The famous image of Śiva in Elephanta, called '*Trimūrti*', is Śiva as *sadāśiva,* as Pārvatī and as *aghora,* the fierce one. Through a juxtaposition of three impersonalized states, a fourth—

that of complete equanimity—is evoked. The multiple faces, the multiple arms, are the artistic expression of this without form, beyond form oneness and unity, which is reflected through a spectrum of multiple forms, each interlocked in a cohesive meaningful structure. In its totality, whether the an-iconical *liṅgam* or the *trimūrti* or the images with many faces, all evoke the response of an aesthetic experience heightened, subtle and chiselled. The sculptural form, the particular stalk of the lotus, the contours of the vegetative creeper, the aquatic and terrestrial animals, the *gandharvas* and *apsaras* and the human form, accompanied by them or in isolation, standing, sitting or lying upon these or serpents, animals or dwarfs, are all now the transient states (*vyabhicāri bhāva*)—all vehicles of a soul state. They are a concrete embodiment of an inner psychic experience of significance and universal validity and meaning. Everything, whether in the sculptural relief or the individual stone or bronze image, the monumental reliefs of Sanchi, Amaravati, Halebid, Belur, Hampi, Konark, are constituents of a cosmic design, almost a geometric diagram or symbols of an impersonalized state, an archetypal dominant mood with its concomitant transient emotions. In turn, the relief or the image evokes an analogous state whether of love *śṛṅgāra* or heroism or valour, of fierceness or humour or sheer joy. One has only to look at the images of the dancing Naṭarāja of Śiva or the figures of Durgā slaying the demon Mahiṣa and the vast variety of Viṣṇu images, to be convinced of the fact that as in architecture, the sculpture begins from a still centre, builds upon a central axis and again makes a construct of expanding circles with diameters, radii, all moving into the centre and moving out of the centre. In short, the theory and technique of plastic expression is based on a system of multilayered correspondences. There is a correspondence between lines, straight, erect, symmetrical, diagonal or curved, spiral or otherwise, and impersonalized mood or emotion, as also between certain proportions and attitudes of standing, sitting and lying and certain moods—dominant or subsidiary. Each part of the relief or each micro-unit of the human figure plays its role—the eyes, nose, ears, face, torso and limbs, and each physical gesture, singly and in combination, is suggestive of an inner meaning which, in its totality, suggests an impersonal emotion and thus evokes a transcendental heightened experience. The content, the particular motif, the style, the costume and coiffure, all have an individuality, enabling the spectator to date and localize these reliefs, images within their cultural boundaries, but the ultimate taste and relish of *rasa* (experience) is trans-cultural or trans-national. Drama evokes *rasa* in time and sequence. Sculpture does it through mass, volume, measure in space.

Painting schools and styles, ranging from those of Ajanta, Ellora to the caves of Bagh and murals of Alchi, give further evidence of this avowed faith and commitment to the impersonalized dominant moods (archetypals) first identified by Bharata, which have been and are expressed in cultural specifics. At one level, there are as many schools of paintings as there are dynasties; at another level, each is the reflector of an impersonalization which has been the beginning and is the ultimate goal. Again, the range is staggering in its multiplicity, ranging from Ajanta to Sittanavasal to even the Islamic geometrical designs. However, once again, in each of these, the archetypal dominant states, the reaching out to infinity and the expression through culture-specific idiom is vital and fundamental. Hindu, Buddhist and Jaina figurative art is as abstract as Islamic calligraphy Lines alone, with or without colour in their use, as straight, terse, diagonal, ascending or descending, curved lines as intertwined spirals or half-crescents, are all symbolic of inner states of mind, dominant and subsidiary emotions: in their totality, whether as figurative art or as abstract lines, they embody the archetypal universal and follow the same principle.

The characters—heroes and heroines of epic poetry and drama—are also archetypes as is the world of flora, fauna, animal or bird life. The mythic image is its universe through a formal language of symbols, signs and motifs; it conveys universal meaning within and outside cultural boundaries. The inner dynamics of the poetry of Vālmīki, Kālidāsa and the isometrical shapes of Islamic calligraphy are comparable. Again, the abstract and the concrete move together. Indian poetry transforms the notion of ecological balances into the recurrent rhythm of the seasons: plant, animal, human, water, earth, fire, sky, are again in dialogue. The passage of annual time, the seasons, acquire deep meaning and so spring, summer, autumn and winter are valid for themselves but more for what they convey beyond themselves. They are all like the sculptures on walls of temples, vehicles and tools for evoking a unified experience. Neither character nor plot is important in itself. They are interwebbed as a labyrinth and drama is always cyclic in nature.

These are the more permanent arts, frozen at a moment of time for posterity. What about the occurrent arts—music and dance, oral recitations and the dramatic experience? They are shaped and formed in the art of creation, live for the moment in specific duration. Now, instead of time being frozen in consecrated space, space is consecrated in time of fixed duration. The beginning and end of the performance in sound or movement is a consecration when the cosmos is made anew for that duration; it is complete and whole, whether of five minutes or two hours or five days' enactment. The beginning is the same—the still centre, the immutable invariable inwardness; the fixed note of the scale or the stances of the dancer. Thereupon is an enlargement in expanding concentric circles of the cosmos, whether through one or three octaves, the exploration of space in all its variety of shades of tonality, micro-units of sound, light, shade, stresses, accents, and discriminating exclusion of particular notes. The edifice is built with sound; it is architectonic in character. Now, both the musician and the listener circumbulates as the pilgrim did the *stūpa,* in clockwise but ascending direction. Through the structured patterning of sound, the multitude of life in its endless variety is presented, and a dominant mood is created; together, the still centre and its flowerings like a lotus petal, evoke the state of heightened aesthetic experience. While the creator-performer begins with the state of internalized *yoga* and expresses through consummate skill the dominant mood, the listener responds by returning to the state of bliss where the artist had begun. Again, impersonalized emotion, a dominant mood, a multiplicity of sound, symbols and motifs combined with intensity create an icon in music which the listener can worship, as he could the sculptural image in stone or bronze. Little wonder that images are called *mantra mūrtis* (images of chants) and music is the ultimate *Nāda Brahman* contained in a single sound 'Aum' or its elaboration.

And finally, through a beautiful and complete language of movement, Indian dance provides the most concrete manifestation of the inner state and vision. The dance, like poetry, music and sculpture, seeks to communicate universal, impersonal emotion and through the very medium of the human form, it transcends the physical plane; in its technique, it employs the technique of all arts and it is impossible to comprehend the architectonic structure of this form without being aware of the complex techniques of the other arts which it constantly and faithfully employs and synthesizes. The themes which the Indian dancer portrays are not only the raw material of literature, but are also the finished products of literary creation; the music which seems to accompany the dance is actually the life-breath of its structure and, indeed, dance interprets in movement what music interprets in sound; the postures and the stances it attains are the poses which the sculptor models; all these the dancer imbues with a living spirit of movement in a composition of form which is both sensuous and spiritual. The body is the medium to transcend the 'body'.

Bharata had inherited a 'vision'; he gave it form as concepts and framework. The creative artist, in turn, internalized the vision of the inner and outer life he had experienced. The principles of structure enumerated by Bharata were inherited directly or assimilated as part of a larger ambience, gave the artist the tools for creating a variegated world of 'forms' and multiple forms only to evoke the beyond form (*pararūpa*).

6

TEXT

The Inflow and the Outflow

To return to the inheritance and lineage of Bharata, as also those who inherited from him—we have already referred to Bharata's indebtedness to the Vedas, the Upaniṣads and Brāhmaṇical *yajña* practices. He incorporates the system of *pūjā* later codified in the *āgamas,* draws freely from contemporary practice, and considers *loka,* the 'people', as the final authority.

His eclectic approach is undeniable. This confluence (*prayāga*)—a big lake or a mini ocean—led to an outflow of many streams at critical and creative levels. In turn, other confluences occurred. The process of the inflows confluences, outflows and re-occurring confluences gave the textual tradition vitality and resilience, with an ability to sustain perennial flow and continuous change.

The question still remains: did Bharata have any predecessors, not as general sources for mythology, thought and structure, but at the level of formulation? Scholars have traced the history of Indian drama to the Vedic dialogues of Yama and Yamī, of Purūravas and Urvaśī. In this respect Bharata only refers to the Purūravas and Urvaśī in the very last chapter (XXXVI) of his work.

We are alluding to that other category of texts which

attempt an exposition of a framework of the formal elements of art or suggest a theory. The *Naṭasūtras* referred to by Pāṇini have been cited as examples. The *Aṣṭādhyāyī* (IV. 3.110–111) refers to them and the schools of Śilālin and Kṛśāśva. Although the works are possibly irretrievably lost, perhaps, this was the first attempt to codify some rules of dramaturgy.

Other than this scanty evidence on which Lévi,[1] Hillebrandt,[2] Weber,[3] Konow,[4] Keith,[5] De,[6] Kane,[7] Ghosh,[8] V.S. Agrawaḷa,[9] have all commented, there is scant evidence of the existence of a 'work' comparable in approach or volume to the *Nāṭyaśāstra.*

The fact that there was a flourishing tradition of poetry, dance and music, even of architecture, sculpture and painting, is evident from innumerable references in the Vedas and epics. Patañjali's *Mahābhāṣya* and *Arthaśāstra,* the *Rāmāyaṇa* and the *Mahābhārata* provide interesting details of theatre halls, recitals, social status and training, but of the works of writers *ācāryas* or *ṛṣis* of the arts we learn little.

Bharata provides a list of his *gurus* (teachers) and contemporaries. Apart from Pitāmaha Śiva and Maheśa, he mentions Kohala, Dhūrtila (Dattila), Śalikarṇa, Bādarāyaṇa (Badari) and others. We know little or nothing of most of them. The name of Śatakarṇi appears in an inscription possibly of the first century BC or AD 149, but no more. All information is from post-Bharata sources, including Kohala whom Bharata mentions in the last chapter. An exception is Dattila or Dhūrtila, the writer of *Dattilam*—a text devoted specially to music, or even a more specific field of *gāndharva* music. The others Bharata refers to, are largely names. Of their works we learn only from secondary material post-Bharata, especially in the great work of Abhinavagupta, namely, the *Abhinavabhāratī.*

From the internal evidence of Bharata and that provided by his successors, it would appear that there was a community of thinkers or theoreticians, but in the absence of the 'manuscripts' no conclusive statements can be made. From the authors quoted by Abhinavagupta who, in turn, quote their predecessors and their works, it would appear that some works were available until the sixth or even the tenth centuries but no more can be added except for the one possible exception of Dattila.

Of the successors, more can be said.

We have, necessarily, to both periodize as also classify the successors under a few broad categories, although neither period nor specific discipline areas have clear-cut boundaries. There is invariably and characteristically much overlap and some ambiguity.

Except Dattila, who was either a predecessor or a contemporary, all others are successors. The rough periods are from the second century AD, more definitely to the tenth century, when Abhinavagupta appears on the scene, and post-tenth century, in some fields, and post-thirteenth century in others (especially, music e.g., a text like the *Saṅgītaratnākara,* and architecture) to the eighteenth century. The textual literature in terms of names from secondary sources is voluminous. However, not many texts have been systematically collated and edited and published. Hundreds of others lie as manuscripts in public or private collections, in India and abroad, and an equal or larger number are in fragments.

From amongst those that have received attention of scholars from the fields of literature, poetics and dramaturgy, music, dance, architecture, sculpture and painting, it is possible to surmise that Bharata's text provided the single unified source for a theory of art. This along with observation and analysis of contemporary practice of each of these arts resulted in several parallel streams of a textual tradition. There were texts on poetics, on dramaturgy, dance as a separate category, architecture, sculpture and painting, together and separate, and special sections of the *Purāṇas* devoted to the arts. All were indebted in part or whole to the *Nāṭyaśāstra*. One last category is that of *āgamas*, difficult to date, but their contents also have relevance to what we may call by the generic term, the *Nāṭyaśāstra* tradition or *paramparā*.

Most of these texts deal with the formal aspects of a single or a group of art forms. It is clear that fairly early after the formulation of the *Nāṭyaśāstra*, already different but related streams began to flow out of the *Nāṭyaśāstra*. These include writers on poetics, dramaturgy, music and dance, architecture, sculpture and painting.

However, from the sixth century onwards (except for some portions of the *Agni Purāṇa* attributed to the fourth by some, ninth century, by others) there was another major development of 'commentators' and interpreters of the *Nāṭyaśāstra*. Their central concern was with the nature of the aesthetic experience, the process of artistic creation and the response of the reader/spectator/audience. It is they who may be called the 'theoreticians' in a more exact meaning of the term. By the tenth century, we encounter the towering figures of Ānandavardhana and Abhinavagupta.

From the tenth century onwards, there are again two principal streams—one of the 'theoreticians', and the other, of writers of particular texts (*śāstras*) of the different arts. Again, the categories are not insulated because when we peruse a work like Bhoja's *Śṛṅgāra Prakāśa*, it encompasses a vast field. The textual tradition continues upto the late eighteenth and in some cases early nineteenth century. The codification of formal elements and the practice (*prayoga*) complement each other and it is no slavish imitation or repetition although borrowings and dependence on earlier sources is frequent and not uncommon.

With this general background, let us look at a very select number of these texts from each field, only to identify a few elements of continuity and change, adherence or departure from the *Nāṭyaśāstra.* The attempt is neither a comprehensive listing or an in-depth analysis of either category or particular texts.

Amongst the first are those in the field of music. We have mentioned that Dhūrtila or Dattila was either a predecessor or contemporary. Mukund Lath, who has made an in-depth study of the text on the basis of the single extant manuscript, believes that the writer was perhaps a predecessor, certainly a contemporary.[10] The work *Dattilam* assumes importance because of its pointed discussion on the category of music called *gāndharva.* The *Nāṭyaśāstra* mentions the term, and distinguishes it from others. *Dattilam* provides different definitions and explanations. According to Mukund Lath *gāndharva* in the *Dattilam* stands for a specific corpus of music. It was a sacred form, parallel in this sense, to the more ancient *sāma* from which it was thought to have been derived. It was basically, like *sāma,* a sung form—though it could also be played. It comprises *pada* (words), *svara* (notes) and *tāla* (rhythm).[11] We will remember Bharata's categorization of the two levels of the divine (*daivika*) and human (*mānuṣī*). This could be applicable here. Bharata also mentions these components. However, a comparison reveals that Bharata's framework and context was the theatre, and Dattila's only music. Other differences are apparent in the hierarchical values of *śruti* and *svara* (intervals and notes) While we may not dwell upon these here, it is important to note that the tradition of textual writing as *śāstra* begins early where particular subjects are taken up, definitions given and specifics analysed. In the sphere of music, the several categories formulated by Bharata continue to be followed over a very long period although their definitions and interpretations vary and some changes are also noticed. In the case of *gāndharva* it receives special attention later from Abhinavagupta.

A major change in the field of music takes place with Mataṅga's *Bṛhaddeśī* (sixth and seventh centuries AD). It is Mataṅga who elucidates the categories of *mūrchhanās*, and *jātis* and introduces the term *rāga* for the first time. It deals at some length with the forms and characteristics of the seven pure *grāma rāgas*. Most significant is his definition of *deśī* and *mārga*, two terms which were to dominate the Indian arts for centuries. Indeed, for him *mārga* is a sub-category of *deśī*. This paradox of categories engages the 'musicologist' and the dramatist alike for many centuries. Mataṅga anticipates Śārṅgadeva in his description of the articulation of sound from different centres of the body. Bharata had mentioned the three locations (*sthānas*) of sound, from the chest, throat and palate. Dattila accepts and Mataṅga elaborates and Śārṅgadeva gives physiological and *tāntric* explanations. Other terms introduced by Mataṅga are significant even though they begin to signify other concepts, principal amongst these being *dhvani* and *nāda*. Both these terms have a long and involved history which is not restricted to music.[12] Premlata Sharma in her annotation of a recently published edition traces the history of development of these terms. Along with the introduction of new categories, the discussion on the primary categories of Bharata's system of *śruti svara grama murchhanās* continues.

A similar tendency is noticed in the most important

text on music, namely, the *Saṅgītaratnākara*[13] (thirteenth century). One life-line is the perennial, i.e. of the *Nāṭyasastra,* the other of change. While in the matter of basic structure he follows the *Nāṭyasastra,* quotes or uses it almost verbatim, specially in the chapter on dance, he incorporates a whole new category of movements, called *desi karanas.* The *Saṅgītaratnākara* elaborates on some concepts which were implicit in the *Nāṭyasastra.* In introducing a category called *deśī,* the text attempts definitions of the other category, called *mārga.* Bharata does not explicitly set up the pair of *mārga* and *deśi* as opposites.

We had mentioned that the concept of the primary elements (the *bhūtas*) is implied in the *Nāṭyaśāstra.* It is the *Saṅgītaratnākara* which elaborates on the genesis of human embodiment in his chapter on the treatment of *svaras* and lucidly presents the relationship of the body, the five primary elements (the *mahābhūtas,* here), with sound, intelligence, etc. (*Saṅgītaratnākara,* verses 56 to 71). A close reading of these verses also convinces one of the intrinsic relationship of the Āyurveda system (specially, Śuśruta and Caraka) and the arts of music and dance. Examples could be multiplied from texts on music (*saṅgīta*) from different parts of the country upto the eighteenth century, which exemplify the phenomenon of both indebtedness as also originality.

We notice three trends, one of adherence to some key principles of the *Nāṭyaśāstra,* another of introduction of new categories and, a third, specially in the second period of the eleventh century onwards, of descriptions of fully developed regional schools and styles. This is a pan-Indian phenomenon. In the case of music, it can be traced through several works, such as the works of *Bharatabhāṣya* of Nānyadeva (twelfth century AD), Someśvara's *Abhilaṣa-*

tārthacintāmaṇi or *Mānasollāsa* (a work which deals also with architecture, music and dance, twelfth century), the *Saṅgītopaniṣat Sāroddhara* of Sudhākalaśa (from Gujarat—fourteenth century), *Saṅgīta Samayasāra* of Pārśvadeva from Karnataka, the *Saṅgītanārāyaṇa* and *Saṅgīta Kaumudī* from Orissa (sixteenth–seventeenth century) and *Saṅgītarāja* of Kumbha (fifteenth century—Rajasthan). The *Ain-e-Akbari* relies heavily on the *Saṅgītaratnākara* in its music and dance chapters. So does the later work—*Risala-i-Rāgadarpaṇa.* Both adherences and changes can be discerned in the later works, such as, *Saṅgīta Mallikā* of Mohammed Shah (seventeenth century) and *Kitabe Nau Rasa* of Adil Shah. Parallel runs the tradition of many Tamil works, beginning with the important commentary on the *Śilappadikāram.* In these texts, there are descriptions of the five *pāns* or geographical areas, seven *palais* or *mūrchhanās* and twenty-one *tirams* or *rāgas.* The basic foundations were laid by Bharata. However, it is Mataṅga's formulations, specially in regard to *grāma* and *rāga* that is adhered to throughout as is evident from later texts, like Ahobala's *Saṅgītapārijāta* (AD 1724). However, in the early part of the nineteenth century we come across the work of a Mohammed Raza (1813) called *Nagamat-e-Ashrafi.* Here, he vehemently questions the *rāga-rāgiṇī* classification. He considers it absurd and meaningless.

From even the few but valuable works mentioned (our list is by no means exhaustive), we can surmise that a distinctively Indian form of music based on the system of micro-intervals (*śruti*) and notes (*svara*) in an ascending and descending order, with consonance, assonance and dissonance, along with a highly complex system of *tāla* develops. Bharata provided a conceptual framework. Mataṅga laid the foundations and a ground plan and others built on it by creating many new forms (e.g., *dhrupad, khayal, ṭappa, thumri, dadra, kṛti, tillāna,* etc.). All in all, while many new regional, sub-regional schools and even individual styles developed, the basic foundation of a 'modal' system of music was not demolished.

The living traditions of the several schools, the *gharanas* and the *sampradāyas* of Hindustani and Carnatic music bear testimony. The continuous flow of the tradition, as also the infinite number of possibilities of change and creativity is obvious.

The case of 'dance' as a separate category of art, distinct from the large landscape of Bharata's *āṅgikābhinaya* (body-language) is similar. Bharata had spoken of *āṅgikābhinaya,* had identified the category of *nṛtta* as pure movement without meaning. He divided it into *tāṇḍava* and *sukumāra* as modes of rendering without specifically relating them to male and female. The *karaṇas* could be performed by either. Nandikeśvara (dated variously between sixth and eleventh centuries), writer of the *Abhinaya-darpaṇa* gives 'dance' the status of an autonomous art. For him now there is a generic category *naṭanam* which he classifies into *nṛtta, nṛtya* and *nāṭya.* For Bharata, *nāṭya* was the generic category. For Nandikeśvara, it becomes a sub-category, although the larger rubric of the form *abhinaya,* he maintains. These changes are of significance as also his division of dance into *tāṇḍava* and *lāsya* and attributing one to male and other to female (Tāṇḍu and Pārvatī as originators).

A perusal of the text[14] also reveals the introduction of two new categories of *hastas* (hand-gestures), namely, the *daśāvatāra hastas* and *nakṣatras* (planets). The absence of these in the *Nāṭyaśāstra* and their presence in the *Abhinayadarpaṇa* is significant. The incorporation of new material and evolution of categories appears as a fairly pervasive phenomenon. The myths of the *daśāvatāra* and performance based on them must have been prevalent for the author to attempt classifying them. There are other significant departures in the matter of descriptions of movements, called *bhramarīs* and *utplavanas*. One denotes pirouettes and the other, elevations from the ground. The text makes no theoretical statements on the nature of the art except in the very first verse where Śiva's 'cosmos' embodying the four *abhinayas* is described. Also, Bharata had divided his *āṅgika* (body) into *aṅga* and *upāṅga*. Nandikeśvara introduces *pratyaṅga*—a term Bharata uses in a different context, but once.

The conciseness of the text was responsible for its wide popularity and the numerous manuscripts. For the practising dancer it became a textual authority for centuries and it is still followed.

Jayasenāpati's *Nṛttaratnāvali* from Andhra (thirteenth century) also reflects both adherence to and departures from the *Nāṭyaśāstra*. While it follows the basic principles, it focuses much greater attention on training *vyāyāma* and a full account of the *deśī* type of *karaṇas*. We gather very important information from this text[15] on many matters, including the basic techniques of training, including those on the bar. Unlike others, he includes a section on construction of theatres. Also, his work is the richest source after Abhinavagupta for a detailed commentary on the *Nāṭyaśāstra*. He was also acquainted with the works of Kohala, Someśvara and Pārśvadeva. The *Pereni nṛtya* and others which have been revived recently, have looked for inspiration from dances described in the *Nṛttaratnāvali*.

We have already referred to Śārṅgadeva's indebtedness to the *Nāṭyaśāstra*. Chapter VII of the text which deals exclusively with dance, leans heavily on the *Nāṭyaśāstra*. His greatest contribution is the evolution of a new category of cadence of movement, called *deśī karaṇa*. He and Jayasenāpati were contemporaries. The two works together establish firmly the legitimacy of a class of music and dance, both called *deśī*.

The most important text which reflects great changes which must have taken place by the sixteenth century, is the *Nartananirnaya*[16] of Paṇḍarīka Viṭṭhala, a Kannad, who lived in the court of Akbar, who was at home both in the north and south. He displays remarkable capacity of eclecticism, incorporates contemporary practice into the textual tradition. He is indebted to Śārṅgadeva and other predecessors, such as Someśvara, for the category of movement called *deśī*. He goes a step further by extending Bharata's classification of musical composition into *nibaddha* and *anibaddha* (structured and unstructured) (*N.S.* XXXII, 28) and applies it to dance. *Nṛtta* (dance) he tells us, is of two kinds: *baddha* (structured) and *anibaddha* (unstructured). He also uses the term *niyam* (rule) rather than *vidhāna*. Although Bharata certainly provides scope for variations and improvizations in all his works, he had not laid out any such categories. A significant departure is in respect of *karaṇas*. Now they have shrunk to only sixteen. Obviously, the tight structured cadence had given place to more fluid movements. Paṇḍarīka, in turn, influences Dāmodara, the writer of the *Saṅgītadarpaṇa* (seventeenth century). The sheer extensiveness of the manuscripts of *Nartananirṇaya* reflects its wide influence and popularity. *Nartananirṇaya* is also interesting from the point of view of a full discussion on anklets (*ghungroos*) and compositional forms such as *jakkadi*, which became popular in the Moghul and Maratha courts in the seventeenth and eighteenth centuries.

The trend of following Bharata, Nandikeśvara and Śārṅgadeva in the matter of basic body-language in dance and yet introduction of new categories of movement with a distinctively regional style, continues. This is evident from texts—*Hastamuktāvali* from Assam, *Abhinayacandrikā* from Orissa, *Hastalakṣaṇadīpikā* from Kerala and many others. The phenomenon of a pan-Indian character as also distinctive regional schools, with one life-line of continuity and the other of change, is evident. A fuller analysis has been attempted earlier.[17]

The texts, as also the practice, of architecture, sculpture and painting are indebted to the *Nāṭyaśāstra* in different ways. We know that the *Nāṭyaśāstra* provides details of the architectural plan and construction of the theatre hall, the stage, the centre and peripheral areas and the free standing pillars.[18] Texts of architecture, as also actual construction, follow the basic grid of the *vāstupuruṣa maṇḍala.*[19] This is as much related to concepts and methodologies of Brāhmaṇical ritual (*yajña*) as to the concept of the *brahma maṇḍala* enunciated in the *Nāṭyaśāstra.* The second chapter of the *Nāṭyaśāstra* must have, no doubt, provided inspiration, if not an immediate model. The fundamentals underlying the conceptual plan and lay out of architectural buildings is similar, if not identical. While actual temples of the early period do not incorporate a *naṭamaṇḍapa,* medieval temples from the south to the east (Cidambaram, Konark) all have *naṭamaṇḍapas.* Their ground plan and, in the case of Konark perhaps elevation plan and pillars are reminiscent of descriptions of the stage in the *Nāṭyaśāstra.* We must remember that the texts on architecture (*vāstu*) are coeval with a great deal of architectural activity and the development of different types of temple types, specially the *Nāgara, Drāviḍa* and *Veśara.*[20]

None of this evidence matches the incontrovertible evidence of the *Kūttambalams* of Kerala.[21] Though late, they are the closest approximation to Bharata's theatre. Thus the texts from the east and the west, *Śilpaprakāśa* and *Silpasāriṇi* from Orissa, *Aparājitapṛcchā* from Gujarat, *Mānasollāsa* from Karnataka, *Samarāṅgasūtradhāra* from Madhya Pradesh *Tantrasamuccaya* from Kerala and others have sections which have a direct relationship with the *Nāṭyaśāstra,* both in approach as also structure. Throughout the discussion in the *Vāstu* texts, the concept of seed (*bīja*), womb (*garbha*) and point (*bindu*) and *puruṣa* as terms of reference are central.

The debt of Indian sculpture (*śilpa*) and *citra* (painting) to the *Nāṭyaśāstra* is at another level. We know that Bharata had not only analysed all parts of the body, but had also categorized both positions and movements. Indian sculpture is based on a system of armature which we recognize by the familiar terms *sūtras* (medians), *mānas* (measures), *bhaṅgas* (positions of symmetry and asymmetry, e.g. *abhaṅga, dvibhaṅga, tribhaṅga*), and *sthānas* (positions of sitting, standing and reclining). The concept of perfect symmetry is indicated by the word *sama,* common to music, dance and sculpture. It has fundamental importance in all the Indian arts and today the most lay of listeners recognize the principle in music and *tāḷa* and in the sculptures of all 'figurative' art (Buddha, Viṣṇu, Śiva alike) when 'quietitude' (*śānta*) or repose is depicted and evoked. Bharata enumerates the principle in several contexts but especially in the context of the primary movements, called *cāris* and the larger movements, called *karaṇas.* There is a whole group of *sama* movements of the parts of the body (*aṅga* and *upāṅga*), but also of the total body. Position and movement emerge from this first stage of 'stasis', balance and repose, and of perfect symmetry. Different degrees of dynamics follow in a variety of configurations of asymmetry.

The *Śilpaśāstras* and Indian iconography develop a

mighty edifice, a pan-Indian vocabulary dealing with *bindu* (point) centre, line, verticals and horizontals, distribution of weight, mass and volume. The affinity between this and the perceptions of the *Natyaśāstra* is remarkable. The distinctive Indian approach of abstracting the body to its essentials of the anatomical structure and establishing a correspondence between centrepoint (navel), verticals and horizontals, coordinating them first with the principal joints of the neck, pelvis, knees and ankles and then with the emotive states, is basic. It was Bharata who first saw this and gave a formal language. The *Śilpaśāstras,* whether directly or from a common original source, adhere to the principle which we recognize so easily as *sama-bhaṅga* of Visnu, Śiva and *abhaṅga* of Kodanda Rama and *tribhaṅga* of Nàṭarāja. The sections on *śilpa* and *citra* in the *Purāṇas,* specially the *Agni* and *Visnudharmottarà Purana,* follow these principles. The chapters in the *Visnudharmottara Purāna* also elaborate on the inter-relationship of the arts [22]

Besides, Bharata had enumerated many standing and sitting positions. All these are incorporated in the *śilpa* texts as also the Purānas. Amongst the motifs, the *salabhanjikā* motif was common to literature, dance and sculpture. Chapter II of Bharata speaks of the other motifs, such as, *vyāla.* All *śilpa* texts devote sections to these motifs. In time to come, a concerted effort is made to arrest in stone the cadences of movement described by Bharata (*cāris* and *karanas*). The walls of Indian temples are replete with the vibrant movement of the dance, as the motifs of the *gāndharvas, kinnaras,* the *śālabhañjikās* and *surasundarīs, alasa kanyās,* heroes combating and *devas* flying. This rich and overpowering vocabulary is the language of Bharata transferred to stone. If the *sàla bhañjikas* and *surasundarīs* recreate the *cāris,* the flying figures recreate the category of *karanas,* called the *vrścika* in Bharata's system.[23] The hundred and eight *karaṇas per se* are all sculpted on the walls of many temples, inner and outer, from Bṛhadīśvara to Palempet, Śārṅgapāṇi,[24] Tiruvanmalai, and in far-off Indonesia on the walls of the Parambanan temple,[25] the earliest of them all.

Each of the *Śilpaśāstras*, the *Agni* and *Viṣṇudharmottara Purāṇa*, in particular, include sections on these aspects.

Here also, there is a pan-Indian unity of vision and perception. There is the evolution of regional schools (not called *deśi* here) with a vast scope for innovation, improvization and change. Whether the rules of *pratimā-lakṣana* were directly derived from the *Nāṭyaśāstra* or not, it is difficult to say, but the basic principles of form have a great affinity. Also, the *rasas* represented on temple walls and the typology of characters and heroes are related to the categories evolved in the *Nāṭyaśāstra.* We may not even list the several texts which speak of the regulations or provide guidelines for depicting 'dance' in sculpture.

Indian painting, mural and miniature, exhibits a distinctive approach to pictorial space and particularly to perspective. We will recall that Bharata had laid down the conventions of spatial division of the stage into different zones (chapter XIII on the *kakṣāvibhāga*). Bharata had also outlined a fairly extensive palette of 'colours' in the matter of dress, make-up, head-dress and crowns. It is these aspects which connect Bharata's text and the rules of composition in Indian painting and the section on painting in the *śilpa* texts as also the *Citrasūtras.* We may refer briefly to the oft-quoted remark on the lack of perspective in Indian painting and no vanishing point. Also, to the frequent comment on multiple moments in time on a single surface (e.g., Indian miniature painting of all schools, some murals also).

Observed more closely, it will be apparent that the

Indian painter was using his defined pictorial surface as the Indian dramatist was using his theatrical space. Multiple scenes could and did take place. The principle of *kakṣāvibhāga* facilitated this. Movement from one area to the other without change of scenes could suggest different locales. Indian painting follows this principle with very few exceptions. This enables the painter to capture different locales by dividing his pictorial space, as also different moments of time, present and past, and even future. The repetition of characters in a narrative in a small area of miniature paintings, specially in the famous sets of the *Rāmāyaṇa* and the *Gīta Govinda* is characteristic.[26] Neither in the matter of figurative art or motifs, is Indian painting is comparable to the pictorial rules of the West. They have to be seen and read from within the pictorial space from the point of view of each character, his outer reaction to another, or his outer movement in different locales, or even deeper, the inner movement of different states of his own being (e.g., Kṛṣṇa or Rādhā in separation and union)

The principles of *kakṣāvibhāga*, and that of the manifestation of (*vyabhicāri bhāva*) transient states, are the two core principles along with a well laid system of colour symbolism of Indian painting. The direct or oblique connection with the *Nāṭyaśāstra* is obvious. The painter divides his pictorial space on the basis of the *triloka* rather than foreground and background. He takes a basic mood and improvizes within the pictorial space. In this respect he is doing what the Indian musician does with the notes in an octave. The *citra* texts imply all this, but do not state it explicitly.

All these arts, singly and together, through their respective texts and practice and their mutual dialogue at both levels, are the multibranched tree of the *Nāṭyaśāstra.* Bharata sowed the seed (*bīja*), but the flowerings were distinct and inter-related. The *Nāṭyaśāstra* does serve as the *kalpa vṛkṣa* tree or the lake we spoke about, for these different shoots to grow into independent trees or as streams to flow, to sustain both a bonding with the source and a continuous dynamism.

We have, with purpose, not referred to the fields of poetics and works on dramaturgy, so far. Their connection with the *Nāṭyaśāstra* is so primary that it would not be necessary to retrace the history of the textual tradition of dramaturgy and poetics. They are the direct inheritors of the *Nāṭyaśāstra*.

So much of value and depth has been written on these texts, ranging from the famous and indispensable *Daśarūpaka* by Dhanañjaya to *Nāṭakalakṣaṇaratnakośa* of Sāgaranandin, and *Nāṭyadarpaṇa* of Rāmacandra and others, that little needs to be added. From a perusal of these texts, it is evident that like their counterparts in music, dance, the writers on dramaturgy were also concerned with the evolution of new categories. From *Abhinavabhāratī* we learn of the category of plays called *Uparūpakas*. Bhoja's *Śṛṅgāraprakāśa* gives us a full description. These texts follow Bharata's basic categories of ten types of plays but add new categories. The *uparūpakas* open a new field which flowers pervasively in all parts of India.

So far, examples largely of the *nāṭaka* have survived. There are, undoubtedly, some outstanding examples also of the *prahasana* and *ḍima*. In epic literature, specially the *Harivaṁśa*, forms like the *hallisaka* and *rāsaka*, are mentioned. However, in critical literature, these later forms were not included in the typologies of plays enunciated by Bharata. The evolution of the category of drama called the *uparupaka* stimulated a renewed popularity of these forms along with a form like the *saṭṭaka*. This provided the foundation of another pan-Indian movement from about the eleventh to the eighteenth or even nineteenth centuries.

The critical texts, especially the *Nāṭyadarpaṇa* of Rāmacandra and Guṇacandra of the Jaina tradition, and the *Nāṭakalakṣaṇaratnakośa* by Sāgaranandin, provide an insight into the nature of the critical discourse in drama. Beside the evolution of typologies of drama, the writers are concerned with the structure of drama, especially the *itivṛtta* (inadequately translated as 'plot'). Sāgaranandin elaborates on the first group mentioned by Bharata, namely, the *avasthā*. In the course of his discussion, he quotes Mātṛgupta—an early commentator from Kashmir. The value of Sāgaranandin's work lies in his critical assessment of the five stages of movement of the *avasthā*, from the point of view of the hero and his application of these structural elements by giving actual illustrations from Sanskrit drama. Bharata had enunciated principles, laid out a framework. His successors apply the principles to creative literature. Rāmacandra and Guṇacandra—the writers of the *Nāṭyadarpaṇa*—are equally concerned with the nature of the *itivṛtta*. They devote a substantial portion of their text to the *itivṛtta*. The text is also important for a re-definition of the re-interpretation of the concept of *sandhis* (juncture). The *Nāṭyadarpaṇa* is one of the few texts which questions the concept of *citrābhinaya* and even *sāmānyābhinaya*. According to the *Nāṭyadarpaṇa*, the *citrābhinaya* can be subsumed in the *āṅgika* and the *sāmānyābhinaya* in the *vācika*. Further, the writers also do not subscribe to Bharata's enunciation of the preliminaries described in the *pūrvaraṅga*. The *Nāṭyadarpaṇa* is of the view that except the *nāndi* (benediction), all others are futile and are meant to deceive the votaries. Obviously, there was a tension between what may be called, the 'Hindu' ritual as distinct from the Jaina tradition.

The *Nāṭyadarpaṇa* and the *Nāṭakalakṣaṇaratnakośa* have many similarities. The *Nāṭyadarpaṇa* appears to be indebted to the *Nāṭakalakṣaṇaratnakośa*, and both are, in turn, indebted not only to Bharata—the fountainhead—but also to Abhinavagupta and Bhoja. We had mentioned that there is a constant movement of inflows, outflows, confluences, independent streams coming together. The textual tradition, along with the practice exemplifies the dynamics of a continuous dialogue. The Sanskrit theatre lived in texts but more in performance of the countless forms of *aṅkiya naṭas, līlas, rāsa, yakṣagānas, bhagavatamelas, māch, nāch, bhāndas* and *nauṭaṅkīs*. This is the history also of the regional languages, dramaturgy and drama, theory and practice, all amalgamated.[27]

The journey from Bhāmaha, Daṇḍin, Vāmana, Ānandavardhana, Mahimabhaṭṭa, Kuntaka to Viśvanātha and Jagannātha in poetics has also been traced and retraced several times, both at the level of discussion on the poetic experience, as also formal elements, specially the relationship of word and meaning (*śabda* and *artha*), qualities (*guṇas* and *doṣas*), *alaṁkāras* and *lakṣaṇas*. These works reveal a great concern with formal elements of prosody and diction in the beginning. This is comparable to some early music works whose concern is with 'specific' forms (e.g., *gāndharva* in *Dattilam*). Perhaps, these were parallel or independent streams outside, preceding or contemporary with the *Nāṭyaśāstra*.

Soon after the composition of the *Nāṭyaśāstra*, either independently or otherwise, a whole school of *alaṁkāraśāstra* emerged. This stream flowed almost separately. Prosody and embellishments were their main concerns. Bhāmaha and Daṇḍin were the two ritualists of poetry. Bhaṭṭa Udbhaṭa followed, but he also commented on the *Nāṭyaśāstra*. Ānandavardhana was the great exponent of *dhvani*, but he did not overlook '*rasa*'. It was Abhinavagupta who once again brought the several streams together. He commented on the *Nāṭyaśāstra* as also the *Dhvanyāloka* (or *Sahṛdayāloka*) in the *Abhinavabhāratī* and *Locana* respectively.

It is through these medieval commentators/interpreters of Bharata that a marked shift takes place in the discourse on poetics. Now, the concern is both with the nature of the aesthetic experience, the quality of the experience, the poetic form, relationship of 'word' and 'meaning', as also the response of the reader and hearer. The dialogue is acutely sophisticated. The quality of the discussions is quite distinct from all that we have so far outlined in the context of the texts in the other arts. The word was primary, and it continues to be so in the tradition of discourse. Understandably, the *kavi* (the revealer) was distinguished from all others. Logically, it is through the 'word' and the faculty of 'reflection' and articulation of the theorists that we have a body of critical writing on the *Nāṭyaśāstra*.

These are the familiar commentators. In fact, they are more. They interpret, theorise and discuss; they are in a dialogical relationship with one another and in many cases the *Nāṭyaśāstra* serves as a springboard for their own theories and positions. They are the intellectuals, conversant and participants in the speculative thought and particularities of viewpoints of the fully developed schools of philosophy (the *darśanas*). They are committed to one or other of these schools—Mīmāṁsā, Sāṁkhya, Yoga, Vedānta, and most important of all, Kashmir Śaivism.

For them the *Nāṭyaśāstra* presents an opportunity to speak of ontology and epistemology. The nature of the phenomenal world is discussed, as also the nature of the experience which is reflected in art, whether the idea or the image is primary, whether the communication is a matter of perception or inference. The issues of specificities and universalization are brought up and the seminal notion of *Sādhāraṇīkaraṇa* (universalization) is introduced into the accepted view that words have two types of power—one, of denotation (*abhidhā*) and the other, of indirect indication (*lakṣaṇā*); a third, of *vyanjana* (suggestion) is added. The last is the power of revelation and illumination and is closest to the more complex notion of *dhvani* (reverberatic ›, suggestion, etc.) Ānandavardhana and Abhinavagupta are the two towering figures who are instrumental in changing the course of the textual tradition. Abhinavagupta's commentary on the *Nāṭyaśāstra,* called *Abhinavabhāratī* and another on Ānandavardhana's *Dhvanyāloka* or *Sahṛdayāloka,* called *Locana,* are the two most indispensable tools for understanding the *Nāṭyaśāstra.* We have made an attempt thus far, perhaps inadequately, to understand the text of the *Nāṭyaśāstra* as a whole without the aid of Abhinava. However, it is Abhinavagupta who illumines and interprets the text of Bharata at many levels, conceptual, structural and technical.

He comments on practically every aspect. In fact, even the 'jungle' of the text of *Abhinavabhāratī* which Ramakrishna Kavi spoke of, is so indispensable that critics have likened Abhinavagupta to a Bradley on Shakespeare or Butcher on Aristotle.

Also, *Abhinavabhāratī* is our only source for discerning the nature of the debate of his predecessors. Most works are lost and except for one single or part manuscript of Udbhaṭa, restored and edited by R. Gnoli, all else has to be reconstructed from *Abhinavabhāratī.* In the next chapter we shall attempt to present a bird's eye view of this discourse of interpretation.

NOTES AND REFERENCES

1. S. Lévi, *Le Theatre Indien,* Paris, 1890, p. 338
2. A. Hillebrandt, *Über die Anjanga des Indischen Dramas,* Munich, 1914, p. 22
3. Weber, *Indische Studien,* Vol. XIII, p. 488
4. S. Konow, *Karpuramañjarī,* 'Introduction', Harvard University Press (MA), 1901.
5. A.B. Keith, *Sanskrit Drama,* Motilal Banarsidass, Delhi, 1992.
6. S.K. De, *History of Sanskrit Poetics,* University of Calcutta, Calcutta.
7. P.V. Kane, *History of Sanskrit Poetics,* Bombay, 1923, p. viii
8. Manomohan Ghosh, *Natyasastra,* Vol. 1, Introduction.
9. V.S. Ag ·wala, *India as Known to Pānini,* Lucknow University, Lucknow,1953.
10. Mukund Lath, *A Study of Dattilam,* Impex India, New Delhi, 1978, p. 61
11. Mukund Lath, *Dattilam,* Indira Gandhi National Centre for the Arts, New Delhi, 1988, 'Introduction' and text.
12. P.L. Sharma, *Bṛhaddeśī,* Indira Gandhi National Centre for the Arts, New Delhi, 1992, 'Introduction' and notes.
13. R.K. Shringy, *Saṅgīta Ratnākara of Śārṅgadeva,* The Adyar Library and Research Centre of the Theosophical Society, Madras, 1943. See 'Introduction' by P.L. Sharma pp. xxvi–xxvii; also see translation of Chapter I by K.K. Raja and Chapter VII by Radha Burnier.
14. Manomohan Ghosh, *Abhinayadarpana, Calcutta Sanskrit series,* Calcutta, 1934.
15. Coomaraswamy and Duggarwala, *Mirror of Gesture;* two different recensions have been used by each of the editors.
16. V. Raghavan, *Nrttaratnāvali of Jayasenāpati, Madras Government Oriental series,* Government Oriental Manuscripts Library, 1965, 'Introduction'.
17. Mandakranta Bose, *Nartananirṇaya,* General Printers and Publishers, Calcutta, 1991; see also his *Nartananiryaṇa,* edited by R. Satyanarayana, IGNCA, Delhi, 1994, See Introduction and text of volume 1, also foreword by Kapila Vatsyayan.
18. Kapila Vatsyayan, *Classical Indian Dance in Literature and the Arts,* Sangeet Natak Akademi, New Delhi, 1978, 2nd edn. pp.33–36
19. Kapila Vatsyayan, *The Square and the Circle of the Indian Arts,* Roli Books. 1983, pp.43–46 on theatre construction; also see K.S. Ramaswami, *Nāṭyaśāstra,* Oriental Institute, Baroda, 1980 2nd edi-

tion, Vol. 1, 'Introduction'; C.B. Gupta, *The Indian Theatre,* Munshiram Manoharlal, Delhi, 1991; Goverdhan Panchal, *Kuttampalam and Kutiyattam,* Sangeet Natak Akademi, New Delhi, 1984.

20. Kapila Vatsyayan, 'Vāstupuruṣa Maṇḍala', *Vistāra,* Festival of India, 1986, pp.116–120. Also see Stella Kramrisch, 'The Temple as Puruṣa', *Studies in Indian Architecture,* edited by Pramod Chandra, American Institute of Indian Studies, Varanasi, 1975; Stella Kramrisch, *The Hindu Temple,* University of Calcutta, Calcutta, 1946.
21. M.A. Dhaky and Michael Meister, *Encyclopaedia of Indian Architecture,* A.I.I.S., Varaṅasi., for details of architectural texts and their application. The subject is too vast to be cursorily treated here. Also see Alice Boner, *Śilpaprakāśa,* translation by Boner, Sharma and Sadāśiva, Brill, Leiden, 1966 pp. xxxi–xlii; Alice Boner, *Vāstusūtra Upaniṣad,* Motilal Banarsidass, Delhi, 1986.
22. H. Sarkar, *The Monuments of Kerala,* Archaeological Survey of India, New Delhi, 1973, p. 81–87. as also for relationship with temple plans.
23. It has not been possible to include even a brief discussion on the indebtedness of the Purāṇas to the *Nāṭyaśāstra.* While the *Vāyu* and *Mārkaṇḍeya* have important chapters on music, the *Agni* and *Viṣṇudharmottara Purāṇa* have voluminous chapters on many aspects, dealt with in the *Nāṭyaśāstra.* The *Agni Purāṇa* discusses matters relating to *rasa, bhāva,* diction as also *aṅga, upāṅga* in chapter 336–346.

    The *Viṣṇudharmottara Purāṇa,* Khaṇḍa III is specifically devoted to sculpture, painting and dance. The dialogue between Vajra and Mārkaṇḍeya unambiguously establishes the inter-relationship of the arts and the primacy of sound and music, (chapters 21–37). Some elucidation of this was attempted in *Classical Indian Dance in Literature and the Arts—Introduction* and chapters I and II pp.19–21
24. Kapila Vatsyayan, 'The Flying Messenger', *Kalākshetra Bulletin.*
25. Kapila Vatsyayan, *Dance Sculpture in Sāraṅgapāni Temple,* Society for Archaeological, Historical and Epigraphical Research, Madras, 1982. An analysis of these sculptural reliefs in terms of Bharata's vocabulary has been attempted.
26. Kapila Vatsyayan, 'The Dance Sculptures of the Lora-Djonggrang (Prambanam)', *NCPA Journal,* Bombay, Vol. VI, No.1, March, 1977.
27. Kapila Vatsyayan, *The Mewari Gita Govinda,* National Museum, New Delhi, 1987. The compositional pattern of the paintings have been

analysed on the basis of Bharata's principles of the Kakṣāvibhāga; Kapila Vatsyayan, *Painting and Dance,* Abhinava Prakashan, Delhi, 1982, Chapter II on Rajasthani paintings.

28. Kapila Vatsyayan, *Traditional Indian Theatre: Multiple Streams,* National Book Trust, New Delhi, 1981. The history of Indian theatre through regional literatures and contemporary performance has been traced here. The same phenomenon of one lifeline of continuity and the other of change can be discerned here. Scholarship in Sanskrit poetics is vast and deep. Kane, De, Raghavan, Krishnamoorthy, Ramachandran, Ingalls Masson and Patwardhan and others, have discussed the subject exhaustively. It was not considered necessary to cover the same ground. Suffice it to say here that while Bharata may or may not have been the inspirer of a whole discipline of Alaṁkāraśāstra and the schools of *rīti*, the relationships and interconnections are not far to seek.

7

The Text and the Interpreters

In the last chapter we had referred to the fact that from the sixth or, more accurately, seventh century onwards, a group of scholars appears, largely from Kashmir, who look at the *Nāṭyaśāstra* at a different level. They are analysts of a very high order.

Sitting on the heights of Kashmir, patronized by the great kings such as Jāyapīḍa (AD 725–761) and Avantivarman (855–883), these intellectuals, philosophers, critics and *sādhakas* reflect on all aspects of the arts, but, particularly poetics and dramaturgy.

They were familiar with the dramas of Bhāsa, Kālidāsa, Śūdraka and Harṣa, the Prakrit poetry of Hāla. Great Śaivite temples had been built and a Kashmiri school of sculpture had come into being. The *Purāṇas* and the mythology were a well understood current language of discourse.

The natural quiet of Kashmir and the security of royal patronage gave time and opportunity for deep reflection.

The text of the *Nāṭyaśāstra* was known; even manuscripts and variants. Singly and together, they commented and interpreted the text, held definite positions and argued their distinctive points of view.

Although some of them commented on a few aspects of the *Nāṭyaśāstra* and Abhinavagupta on all aspects of the text, we shall confine ourselves here only to the relative position of each of these in regard to the central concept of *rasa, sthāyibhāva* and *rasaniṣpatti.*

To come then to the arguments of the principal commentators of the *Nāṭyaśāstra* until we come to *Abhinavabhāratī* by Abhinavagupta. Let us briefly state their inter-related but distinct positions in respect of the core issue of *rasa,* as the aesthetic experience from the point of view of the artist, the aesthetic/artistic object, and the evocation of a similar, if not identical, experience in the aesthete/receptor or audience.

Bharata, as has been pointed out repeatedly, only lays down the general parameters of the presentation of *rasa* through *sthāyi bhāva,* the determinants (*vibhāva*) and stimulants (*anubhāva*). These are elaborated upon through the transient and contingent states (the *vyabhicāri* or *sañcāri bhāvas*). Inherent in this exposition is the first demand of impersonalization and abstraction. Life-phenomenon itself is abstracted into the principal categories of love, pathos, heroism, fierceness, laughter/humour, jealousy, disgust, fear, wonder, etc.—all ultimately leading to equanimity and harmony. The artist/creator at the very initial inception begins from a psychic state of undifferentiation and unmanifest. This experience is manifested through abstract emotive categories. This is the world of differentiation (the eight *rasas*). We have commented earlier on how the word *anukaraṇa, anukīrtana, anukathana,* cannot be equated to the English word (or its Aristotelian or even Platonic nuances) imitation or mirroring the world from any specific idealized or real-life models.

Abhinavagupta's *Abhinavabhāratī* is our only source for discerning the views of the early commentators, specially Bhaṭṭa Lollaṭa, Śrīśaṅkuka and Bhaṭṭa Nāyaka and Bhaṭṭa Tauta. The views of these writers have to be understood against the background of the evolution of distinct schools of Indian philosophy (*darśana*) principally Mīmāṁsā, Sāṁkhya, Yoga, Vedānta and Kashmir Śaivism. Each of the commentators was investigating Bharata's exposition of *rasa* and *sthāyibhāva* from the tacit assumptions of their particular schools of philosophy. The discourse on the nature of aesthetic experience, creation, presentation, expression and the evocation of an analogous experience in the receiver is also a dialogue of the philosophic schools, on the nature of the phenomenal world. Questions on what constitutes the 'real' are raised and discussed.

Bhaṭṭa Lollata concentrates his attention on the question : 'Where is *rasa* or where does *rasa* reside?'. At a simple or even superficial level, his answer is that *rasa* is not in the visual or verbal presentation by the writer or actor, but, indeed, in the 'idea' which the writer grasps. To the question whether *rasa* is in the 'idea' of Rāma or in the verbal description of Rāma or the actors' presentation of Rāma or the painting of Rāma, the answer is that it is in the abstract idea of Rāma in the mind of the writer or artist. The 'actor' identifies or recreates this 'idea' so as to produce a mental construct which corresponds to the original 'idea'. The logical question would be: whether the original 'idea' has an objective existence of its own or is itself formed at the very moment of conception in the mind of the artist, but, prior to giving it shape and form in words or line or 'colour' or 'sound'. Bhaṭṭa Lollaṭa uses a highly contextually loaded term of Śaiva philosophy, namely, *anusandhāna* which had a close relationship to the word *yojana.* The artist's concern is an attempt to present and communicate the idea, the unified idea, so as to say, through multiple means or configuration of emotive states and situations, mimetic changes and transient emotions. The basic emotive (mental) state *sthāyibhāva* provides the thread of unity to the entire process of creating the artistic form. In contemporary language, shorn from the contextual vocabulary, Bhaṭṭa Lollaṭa's concern is with the process of the creation of artistic form and how the particular artistic form corresponds to the birth of the 'idea' in the creator and artist. If Bharata had used the words '*anukaraṇa*' and '*anukathana*' in explaining the process of the creation of 'form' in the sense of re-statement, re-narration, Bhaṭṭa Lollaṭa uses the word *anusandhāna* and *yojanā*. He brings into the discussion an element of both deep reflection and will and effort needed to create that 'form' which will correspond to the perfect 'form' or perfect 'idea' at the moment of conception. Śaiva philosophy, specially Utpalācārya in the *Īśvara Pratyabhijña Kārikā* speaks of *pūrvābhāsa yojanā*, an incipient experience and a refined sensibility (*samskārāt kalpanā proktā*). Bhaṭṭa Lollaṭa extends the argument to the nature of the aesthetic presentation to suggest that there is a causal relation between the 'idea', the specificity of the form and the principal emotive state, in the same manner as there is between a mystic transcendental experience and its presentation or suggestion through a concrete symbol. Interestingly, three distinct levels are being suggested. The first is the mental, state of mind of the artist/writer where a unified experience takes place. The second is the process of giving form to the experience again, by accepting an abstracted type of form and, third, of a process of creating a multiplicity of situations, stimulants and variations, only with a view to communicate the original unified experience of the artist.

Traditional Sanskrit scholarship has considered Bhaṭṭa Lollaṭa's theoretical position as an important, but not original contribution to the understanding of Bharata's chapters on *rasa.* A closer examination of the passages in the *Abhinavabhāratī* reveal that Bhaṭṭa Lollaṭa was pointing at the source of inspiration and imagination, and the process of artistic creation.

Within the tradition, as discerned from *Abhinavabhāratī*, Bhaṭṭa Lollaṭa was criticized for having ignored in his discussion the last but essential component in the artistic phenomenon, that of the experience of the receptor/spectator/audience. The criticism went further to state that if what was 'expressed' was only a 'symbol', a co-ordinate, worse an illusion, then, how could it have the power or potency to communicate or evoke the image of the original idea in the spectator.

Without going into the details of this criticism, suffice it to point out here that Śrīśaṅkuka, the chief objector of Bhaṭṭa Lollaṭa's interpretation of Bharata's aphorism was at pains to point out that *rasa* was not merely a matter of presentation of 'idea' in specific form or of a historical character on stage but its ultimate efficacy lay only if an ultimate aesthetic experience could be evoked in the spectator. Śrīśankuka made an important contribution to the discussion on *rasa* by pointing out explicitly that *rasa* was not an aesthetic object (abstract 'content', 'theme' in our language) but *rasa* was also and even more important, the aesthetic experience in the receptors', spectators' consciousness. He, thereafter, investigates the question of whether the response of the receptor/spectator is identical/analogous to that of the writer/creator/actor/painter and what is the process of creating the response? Stated differently Śrīśaṅkuka investigates the problem, that if the content of 'art' is already an abstracted category (*sthāyibhāva*) of an even earlier unified category of *rasa*, then, what is recreated in the spectator and how is it re-evoked? His answer is that obviously, if the principal content and form is abstracted, not specific, and that the artist, writer presents it through a variety of tools of situations and stimulants and variations, then, the 'identical' of the original was not possible. The spectator or receptor does not receive the 'identical' or the original. Instead, he infers from the 'forms' of the created artistic image the original and, therefore, has the potential and possibility of a similar but not identical experience as the creator/writer. The psycho-epistemic approach of Śrīśaṅkuka is obvious. He is concerned with the (i) nature of the object of the aesthetic experience, (ii) the means of cognizing it, and (iii) the final response and its nature.

The theory may be considered as one which is based on considering the artistic expression as 'illusion' and not 'real' and one from which only inferences can be drawn. His method of argument adopts the system of *Prācīna Nyāya* (logic). He applies the notions of the nature of reality and knowledge as objective or subjective, the employment of objective tools for cognizing the reality and the method of linking the subject and object to the field of aesthetics. It is interesting to observe how Śrīśaṅkuka carefully applies the principles of (i) *pramātṛ,* the cognizing subject, (ii) *prameya,* the object of cognition, (iii) *pramiti,* the resulting state of knowledge, (iv) *pramāṇa,* the means and measure of knowledge and finally the relationship of subject and object to elucidate Bharata's concepts of *rasa* and *sthāyi bhāva* and *vyabhicāri bhāvas.*

His argument can be restated explicitly by pointing out that he goes to Bharata himself when he focusses on the fact that the state (mental or emotive state, i.e. *sthayı bhāva)* is the underlying principle of *rasa* and is not the object presented. The two examples he gives are important. Just as the painted horse is not the horse, but is the idea of the horse in specific form and yet leads to the cognition of the horse and just as the fear from a rope can arouse the emotion of the fear from a serpent, the artistic creation, although not real or actual, can arouse the experience of the idea of the original in the mind of the spectator. The process is inferential and indirect, rather than of direct perception. It is significant that amongst the commentators, Śrīśaṅkuka is perhaps the first to take pointed cognizance also of the visual image, even if only as analogy, rather than either the verbal text or the performative act. For us today this discussion is important when we realize that a definite change in interpretation of Bharata is visible from that of Bhaṭṭa Lollaṭa. The discussion moves from the performance (actor) to the writer, poet (verbal text) to the painted image even if only as analogy. It is obvious that the field of discussion was being enlarged from the theatre arts to those of poetics on the one hand and the visual, on the other. Also, it is Śrīśaṅkuka who introduces the notion of *alaukika jñāna* in the theatre. In short, the knowledge gained here is different in quality from that in life.

As was to be expected, Śrīśaṅkuka's interpretation was challenged and criticized. His critics understood his theory as one of 'imitation'. To take the analogy of the horse, it was said that the painted horse is an imitation of an actual horse because it bears similarity to the original horse; however, the artistic expression (form) is not portraying a horse; it is conveying, suggesting an idea of a horse. It is more so in the case of the emotive states i.e. *sthāyi bhāva*. Thus, they argued, in its very nature the image on its own cannot be a reflection of the original idea. No one-to-one correspondence could be established between the original idea and the emotive state, between the image (horse, hero, actor) and the response of the spectator. Into this discussion was brought in the 'thin' but important distinction between the concept of *anukaraṇa* (re-narrating, re-presenting or just formulation) and that of *anuvyavasāya* (literally the process of conducting the business of creation or recreation).

The philosophic stream of Sāṁkhya also attempted to interpret Bharata from its particular standpoint. A causal relationship between the presented, concretized form and the emotive state was sought to be established. The concretized form is the external and outer manifestation of an inner experience of pain and pleasure. Art was the interplay of stasis and dynamism as the phenomenal world is of *puruṣa* and *prakṛti*. Hiriyana elucidates this in his book *Art Experience*.

Whatever the minute differences between these varying points of view, it is clear that at the core of the concern and the discussion was the dialectics of the unified undifferentiated experience, its latent capacity of being manifested in 'form' specific and concrete while continuing to be the carrier of a unified, sustained, dominant state (for facility, 'mood'). This interplay of the abstract and concrete, of the nucleus, the 'idea', or ideational and the manifestation in multiple forms and the potential of the multiple forms and the variations to suggest and evoke an experience which is trans-personal, detached and unified is central. The Vedic and Upaniṣadic echoes are clear even if they are now heard in the language of Sāṁkhya or Vedānta.

At this stage (eighth to tenth centuries) many detailed and mutually opposing classificatory systems developed, although there is no break from the perennial life-line of the earlier speculative thought.

After Śrīśaṅkuka, many important developments take place. Śaiva metaphysics is systematized and develops as a powerful system. Utpaladeva writes a detailed commentary—the *Vivṛti*—on the *Īśvara Pratyabhinjña Kārikā*. Śaiva monism (*advaita*) is fully articulated and Ānandavardhana expounds the theory of *dhvani*. The interpretation of Śaiva philosophy into Bharata's aesthetics results in a full-fledged theory of arts.

We know that Śaiva metaphysics posits the conception of a totality and wholeness, an absoluteness, and lays down a hierarchy of stages to attain or experience this totality or undifferentiated stage. The unmediated final state of *anupāya* is reached or possible through the successive stages of *anava* (individual knowledge or perception), *śākta* (divine power) and *sasyabhāva* (divine knowledge or perception). These correspond to *aṇu* (the soul), *śakti* (divine power) and Śiva. Both Ānandavardhana and Abhinavagupta develop a theory of aesthetics on the premise that 'art' is another path for the same goal of experiencing, if not permanently attaining the absolute freedom of universal and unmediated (*anupāya*) consciousness.

Some details of their theories we shall shortly outline. However, at the moment when an unambiguous metaphysics was being developed, arrived Bhaṭṭa Nāyaka, a contemporary or immediate predecessor of Abhinavagupta (approx. AD 883-902). He wrote an important work called *Hṛdyaḍarpaṇa* which is unfortunately extinct. He purposefully followed the Vedāntic school and undertook to decry, if not demolish, the theory of Ānandavardhana and his predecessors. From what we can discern from the excerpts, in the course of his commentary on the very first verse of the *Nāṭyaśāstra*, he refers to the conception of the phenomenal world as expounded by Vedānta. He points at the similarity between it and the dramatic presentation. Just as Brahman (the 'totality' and 'absolute') does not shed its essential nature in the very act of creating the phenomenal world, the world of art (drama) is the manifestation through name and form (*nāma* and *rūpa*) of a multitude of images, without abandoning the essential nature of the original experience. He rejects the inferential theory of Śrīśaṅkuka and asserts that the cognizing self and the cognized object are free from all limitations which give individuality. He incorporates the Vedāntic conception of *ānanda* as the predominance of pure *sattva* (refined, pure, subtle) free from the impurities of the other two attributes of *rajas* (active, horizontal) and *tamas* (inert, dark, gross). For him the aesthetic experience is akin to the mystic experience of Brahman. His contribution to the discourse is seminal. He introduces the concept of *sādhāraṇīkaraṇa.* He also introduces the concepts of the three *guṇas* (qualities) in a very pointed fashion. Also, Bhaṭṭa Nāyaka resumed the debate on the denotation qualities of the word. He was of the view that denotation (*abhidhā*) assumes a new dimension in a second semantic operation where it is freed from all limitations. This he called *bhāvanā,* the aesthetic efficacy of a combination of determinants and consequences. This aesthetic *bhāvanā* had the power for realizing or bringing about a *rasa.* A third stage begins of enjoyment or relish (*bhoga*). For him this is the power of art (language) to universalize and unify and merge the qualities of *rajas* and *tamas* and uplift them to the state of the *sattva.* An ascending order from the gross to the subtle, from the inert to the highly charged and universal is suggested. Bhaṭṭa Nāyaka pays great attention to the last of these three powers, technically called *bhojakatva.* This is the power of freeing from individuation and limitation that makes the work of art have the potential to rise above pain and pleasure, desire or suffering. The artistic work embodies and, in turn, stimulates, a state of awareness and consciousness which is akin to the experience of Brahman. It is unlike the ordinary experience, but is also not identical with the mystical experience, because it is both momentary, and there is but a subsequent recollection of the aesthetic experience.

The aesthetic experience thus, is of the universal aesthetic object being universalized subject in a state of beatitude (*ānanda*) on account of the predominance of *sattva*. Obviously, there can be no experience of *ananda* (bliss) so long as individuality persists.

It will be clear from the brief enumeration that Bhaṭṭa Nāyaka moves away radically from his predecessors, specially Bhaṭṭa Lollaṭa and Śrīśaṅkuka, by shifting the focus of discussion from the nature and process of the artistic object (expression, forms) and the reference of the spectator to the nature of the aesthetic experience, *per se.*

Had Bhaṭṭa Nāyaka's original work *Hṛdayadarpaṇa* or *Sahṛdayadarpaṇa* survived, an important phase of interpreting Bharata would have been clearer.

To take only one example, we have alluded to the seminal importance of the very first verse of the *Nāṭyaśāstra* regarding the origin and nature of drama. Bhaṭṭa Nāyaka gives a most convincing explanation:

> 'I shall (now) expound that drama which was promulgated by Brahman—the highest Self—as an illustration such that people might understand that worldly objects are insubstantial (*nissārabheda*), fabricated (as they are) by ignorance (of the identity between the Self and Brahman) Just as the unreal actions of Rāma, Rāvaṇa and others, which are essentially a figment of one's imagination and hence do not possess a single fixed form, but in a moment assume hundreds and thousands of forms; which though different (in their unreality) from dreams, etc., are still the outcome of mental imagination (*hṛdaya-grahaṇidāna*); which are enacted by actors who are

almost like the creator of the world (Brahma) and who have not relinquished their separate identity (as persons in real life)—those actions (of Rāma and Rāvana, etc.) appear (to us) in a most unusually wondrous way; and though appearing like that, they become the means of attaining the (four) goals of life—in exactly the same way this universe consists of a display of unreal forms and names and yet through listening to and meditating on spiritual instruction, it leads to the realization of the highest goal of human life (namely *mokṣa*).'[1]

Again, Bhaṭṭa Nāyaka speaks of the higher purpose of drama when he declares:

'I pay my homage to Śiva the poet (also the omniscient one—*kavi*) who has created all the three worlds and thanks to whom (*yataḥ*) (sensitive) people are able to attain aesthetic bliss by watching the spectacle (*prayoga*) of the play that is our life in this world.'

We can identify here the interpenetration again of realm of speculative thought and art, the world as drama with the individual as actor and the illusion of drama and illusion of existence. Śiva as the cosmic poet is the eternal creator and destroyer of illusion.

Prima facie, Bhaṭṭa Nāyaka had set out to demolish or decry the theory of *dhvani* as enunciated by Ānandavardhana in his great work *Dhvanyāloka* or *Sahṛdayāloka.* In fact, what he succeeded in doing was to uplift, in a manner of speaking, the notions of the power of word for suggestion (*dhvani*: reverberation) to that of *bhāvanā* (experience of feeling with intensity). Also, he laid the foundations for what was to follow in the works of the great towering personality of Abhinavagupta. The latter was indeed indebted to Bhaṭṭa Nāyaka for many concepts, acknowledged or not, particularly, those of univerzalisation (*sādhāraṇīkaraṇa*) and elucidation of *śanta rasa*.

Abhinavagupta, the towering figure, arrives on the scene with a visionary mind and as one who combines in himself the experience of a mystic, a practitioner of *tantra* and incisive intellectual powers of a philosopher, and the extraordinary skills of a commentator and art-critic. Psychological or psychical human experience is now placed at the centre. Without the all-inclusive universal consciousness, technically called 'Maheśvara', neither perceptual experience nor remembrance is possible, he declared. Utpalācārya was also responsible for the new point of view, that of *ābhāsa*, i.e. the phenomenological, for the study of the problem of *experience*.

Abhinavagupta was deeply indebted to him as also to his other teachers and contemporaries, specially Lakṣmaṇagupta, Bhaṭṭa Indurāja and Bhaṭṭa Tauta. The latter two enabled him to comment extensively on Ānandavardhana's *Dhvanyāloka*. Although students of the *Nāṭyaśāstra* have concentrated on the *Abhinavabhāratī*, the other works, both *Īśvara Pratyabhijñā Vimarśinī* and the *Dhvanyāloka Locana* are equally important for assessing his unique contribution to the history of Indian aesthetics as commentator, elucidator and critic of Bharata.

Abhinavagupta, as has been briefly remarked earlier, was not only immersed in Kashmir Śaivism; he self-consciously extends and applies the philosophic principles to the field of aesthetics. While it would be impossible to adequately summarize the core principles, attention may be invited to a few relevant to his interpretation and elucidation of Bharata and his own distinctive view of the nature of aesthetic experience and art creation.

Brahman (Ultimate Reality) in the Vedāntic conception was *śānta* (quiet, perfect restfulness, without activity), thus static and not dynamic. It was (is) indeterminate (*nirvikalpa*) to be self-luminous (*śuddha cinmātra*). It does not admit of self-consciousness. Kashmir Śaivism, on the other hand, holds that the Absolute is not only self-luminous, but is also self-conscious and dynamic. It argues that the Absolute is that unity which is grasped in a mystic experience but not a mundane experience. It is at a subtle level and similar to *parā vāk* (the transcendental level) and, as such, is free from determinancy and continues to be *nirvikalpa.* The two aspects of self-luminosity (*śiva* or *prakāśa*) and self-consciousness (*śakta* or *vimarśa*) are best figuratively understood in the conception of *Ardhanārī Naṭeśvara* or *Ardhanarīśvara.* The two conjoined—the one as two and inseparable.

The Absolute manifests itself in multiplicity while never shedding its real and potential identity with the Absolute. Thus, the entire world of experience—whether unity or diversity, or diversity and unity, subjective or objective, is the manifestation of Absolute, free will, which is the Ultimate Reality (*svāntantryavāda*) of Kashmir Śaivism.

In order to explain the relationship of the world of manifestation and multiplicity with the Absolute, the analogy of the relationship of the sun and the rays is given. The manifestation is connected with manifesting the Absolute, as rays are to the source of the flame or the sun. All multiplicity is from an unified source of a single universal consciousness. The objective world of manifestation and form can have no more autonomous identity than a reflection can from a mirror or a dream from the dreaming subject. Further, the relationship is acausal; it is the essential nature (*svabhāva*) of the Absolute Will to manifest itself just as it is the sun's essential nature to shine and to emit rays.

Having viewed the nature of the Absolute as the Ultimate principle, Kashmir Śaivism goes on to observe phenomena from the point of view of the manifested variety. In the Absolute, the entire variety is latent and is in a state of perfect unity in the same manner as the variety of the colours of the peacock is in the yolk of its egg. The analogy is so frequently used that it assumes the technical appellation of '*Mayūrānanda rasa nyāya*'. Now all that emanates, is manifested, is called *ābhāsa* which admits of some imperfection or limitation. Even Śiva—the highest category—is an *ābhāsa,* because it represents some disturbance or movement from the perfect quiet and repose. It is the moment of making visible the Absolute (so that the self-luminosity is experienceable). The experience and consciousness implies a 'self' and 'I' and, therefore, the Absolute is both self-luminous and self-conscious. There can be no consciousness without the self and no self without consciousness. Consciousness, thus, is the capacity of awareness of the self, technically called *śakti.*

This central philosophical principle guides Abhinavagupta in explaining the nature of the aesthetic experience. For Abinavagupta, the aesthetic experience is *ānanda,* re-echoing the *Taittirīya Upaniṣad*'s dictum of '*raso vai saḥ*'. Like the Absolute, it is self-luminous and self-conscious, devoid of all duality and multiplicity; it emerges from a single unified source which has the potency of multiplicity. The aesthetic experience is different from any ordinary experience as it is not based on objective perception, but is a subjective experience and realization. Its nature is *alaukika* (trans-mundane) and is akin or analogous to the mystic experience.

It is in the context of the nature of the mystic experience, that the crucial word of Śaiva philosophy, *camatkāra* (in a flash, lightning), is applied to the realm of aesthetics Utpalācārya had used the word in the context of the essential nature of the Absolute as self-luminous (*prakāśa*) but without *vimarśa* (freedom of will). The word '*camatkāra*' is substituted for *vimarśa*. Abhinavagupta elaborates on its metaphysical and aesthetic implications. *Camatkāra* is consciousness of the self, free from all limitations and is also self-luminous (*prakāśa*). This is *ānanda*. The emphasis is clearly on the process of freedom from limitation and points at universalization and a state of 'beatitude' where the 'experience' and not the objective phenomenon of individual unity is of relevance. Many similes and metaphors are used to make explicit the nature of the aesthetic experience. While on the one hand it is akin to the mystic experience, it is also like the experience of tasting a meal or the residual taste of a meal. It is literally mastication, rumination (*carvaṇā*). Bharata had used the word *vyañjanā* and had spoken of the aesthetic experience as the indistinguishable relish and taste of a meal with multiple flavours, but with one lasting residual flavour. Abhinavagupta elaborates and introduces into the critical discourse the key words of *camatkāra parambhoga* and *carvaṇā*. He also incorporates Bhaṭṭa Nāyaka's term of universalization i.e. *sādhāraṇīkaraṇa*.

Śaiva philosophy and Śaiva practice had laid out a well-defined sequence of the ascending scale from the self-individuated self '*aṇu*' to Śakti, to Śiva or Maheśvara. The phases as we have referred to earlier were (*aṇu*), Śakti and Śiva-Sadāśiva or Maheśvara. With great discreetness and sensitivity these categories are extended or applied to the interpretation and elaboration of the process of how the aesthetic experience comes about. First, he illumines the nature of the aesthetic experience and asks the question what is it? And second, Abhinavagupta tells us of how the aesthetic experience is created. Naturally, Bharata's categories of *sthāyibhāva*, the dominant emotive states, the *vibhāvas, anubhāvas* and *vyabhicāri bhāvas* are examined, to elucidate the process.

Further, the three impurities in Śaiva philosophy comprise (i) innate ignorance (*āṇavamala*) which conceals the real nature of the soul, and implies the absence of the consciousness of universality; (ii) indefinite desire (*karmamala*) which implies an objective reference and presupposes imperfection—it is responsible for the countless association of the self with the creation of *māyā*; and (iii) the psycho-physical limitation (*māyīyamala*) where the self is in bondage or limited by *kāla* (division); (iv) *niyati* (determinacy), *rāga* (passion, attachment); (v) *vidya* (information here), *kāla* (time). A movement from the limitless to the limited, from *mahat* to *pṛthvī* is suggested.

Discipline is required for becoming purified from these impurities and limitation, and several paths are suggested, viz. of *kriyopāya,* chanting of *mantras, manopāya* (contemplation) *icchopāya* (exercise of will) and of *anupāya* (grace). All this is necessary for the experience of Maheśvara, (the Absolute). The Absolute, has the power of knowledge of action and abstraction or concretization. Thus, when the Absolute concretizes and the universal, unlimited and undifferentiated, gets limited, it has the attributes and qualities of (i) *sattva,* (ii) *rajas,* and (iii) *tamas.*

This cluster of concepts of Śaiva philosophy which takes into account the process of relationship of the source—the Absolute—to the varying degrees of grossness and subtlety, impurities and imperfection, was excellent ground for investigating and interpreting the key notions of the *Nāṭyaśāstra,* of *rasa, sthāyibhāva* and *vyabhicāri bhāva.* In life the purified state was that of Śiva or Maheśvara. In art the purified state of undifferentiated experience was *rasa* or *ānanda. Sthāyibhāva, vibhāva, anubhāva* and their subcategories of *uddīpana* (stimulants) and *ālambana* (ancillaries), the transient *vyabhicāri* or *sañcāri bhāvas,* were the manifold stages. They were the 'rays' of the sun. In Bharata's world of drama, these singly and together, at multiple levels and through a careful 'phasing' and sequence, could evoke the pure state of bliss (*rasaniṣpatti*). Abhinavagupta examines the concepts with consummate skill, never forgetting that these were the multiple manifestations and tools of diversity. He explores and investigates the process of the one becoming many and returning to the state of perfect unity. equanimity, a state of quietitude and grace (*viśrānti*). However, he makes a clear distinction between the dramatic universe and that of ordinary life. He takes great pains to explain that the very notion of *vibhāva* (determinants) and *anubhāva* (consequents) belong to the dramatic universe. In life, we recognize them by the simple words of 'cause' and 'effect', of *kāraṇa* and *kārya.*

Further, he explains how the *vibhāvas* and *anubhāvas* have been purified, cleansed so as to say, from their association with everyday life; the process of being liberated from bondage or limitation of *kāla* (division) and *rāga* (attachment) and immediate time specificity.

The artistic process is, thus, analogous to the movement of moving from impurity to purity, from grossness to subtlety, from individuation to universality, from multiplicity to unity. Abhinavagupta rejects the 'inference' theory. However, he fully assimilates the principle of universalization, *sādhāraṇīkaraṇa,* of Bhaṭṭa Nāyaka in his formulation as it fits in admirably in his total viewpoint.

Although one could elaborate on the many illuminating passages of the *Abhinavabhārati* and the views of Abhinavagupta on the aesthetic experience and the artistic process, it would suffice here to draw pointed attention to the fact that with such a philosophic view it was but natural and logical for Abhinava to consider the *śānta rasa* as central. Whether Bharata (in some manuscripts there is a section) mentioned eight or nine *rasas* is too long and involved a debate for our purpose here. It is necessary to underline the fact that Abhinavagupta's philosophic position and his discussion on *śānta rasa* are interwebbed. While others, before and after, had considered *śānta* (peace, tranquillity, quietitude) as an additional mood or sentiment, for Abhinava it was the one attribute which permeated all else and to which all else in drama moved. *Hṛdayaviśrānti* was his term.

Closely related and emerging out of this was his elucidation on the spectator/audience/receptor. *Sahṛdaya* was the initiated spectator, one of attuned heart. Brilliantly, he sums up his whole conception in a single para:

> 'The artistic creation is the direct or unconventionalized expression of a feeling of passion 'generalized', that is, freed from distinctions in time or space and therefore from individual relationships and practical interests, through an inner force of the artistic or creative intuition within the artist. This state of consciousness (*rasa*) embodied in the poem is transferred to the actor, the dancer, the reciter and to the spectator. Born in the heart of the poet, it flowers as it were in the actor and bears fruit in the spectator.'
>
> 'If the artist or poet has the inner force of the creative intuition, the spectator is the man of cultivated emotion in whom lie dormant the different states of being, and when he sees them manifested, revealed on the stage through movement, sound and decor, he is lifted to that ultimate state of bliss, known as *ānanda*.'[2]

Lastly, we must perhaps mention the obvious and well-known divisions of the three powers of *sakti,* of *parā, parāparā* and *aparā.* Abhinava tacitly applies these categories in his interpretation of Bharata throughout.

In the Trika philosophy the Divine Consciousness is identical with the Supreme Word (*parā vāk*) and hence each word, every letter is inseparable from this Divine Consciousness.

In such a view, naturally, the 'word' (*vāk*) is symbol supreme which mediates from the mystical dimension to grammar and phonetics, from meaning denotational to 'suggestive' to experience, ruminated. Extended to the whole universe of theatre, naturally, both the 'creator' and the 'spectator' were participants in a 'transmundane' unique experience (*alaukika*) which was none other than the 'flash-like' momentary glimpse of 'I-consciousness' of the 'divine' and had to lead to *hṛdayaviśrānti* (quietitude, tranquility).

The arguments and the discourse is conducted at multiple levels, with a sophistication unparalleled.

The works of both Ānandavardhana (whose *Dhvanyāloka* we could not consider) and Abhinava are important also for the importance they give to the poet. Two verses of Ānandavardhana have been oft quoted:

'In the shoreless world of poetry, the poet is the unique creator. Everything becomes transformed into the way he envisions it.

If the poet is emotionally moved (lit. 'in love') in his poems, then the whole world is infused with *rasa.* But if he be without an interest in the senses (*vītarāga*), then everything will become dry (*nīrasa*).

(*Dhvanyāloka,* III. 43)

Abhinavabhāratī, Volume 1, p. 294 and again

Even though subjects may have been already used,

thanks to the fact that they are associated with imaginative experience (*rasa*) in literature, they all appear new, just as trees appear new during the honey-months (spring).

Thousands upon thousands of poets as eminent as Vācaspati himself might use (various) subjects (in their poetry), and yet, like primordial world-matter, they cannot be exhausted.'

(*Dhvanyāloka*, IV. 10)

But of equal significance is Abhinavagupta's comparing the poet to the creator Prajāpati.

'The poet is like Prajāpati, from whose will this world arises. For the poet is endowed with a power to create wondrous and unheard of things. This power arises from the grace of *parā vāk* ('highest speech'), which is just another name for poetic imagination (*pratibhā*), which has its seat in the poet's own heart, and which is eternally in creative motion (*udita*).'

(*Abhinavabhāratī*, Volume 1, p. 4)

The foregoing discussion, even if a brief and perhaps inadequate account of the many complex issues raised of the principal commentators and interpreters of *Nāṭyaśāstra*, will make it clear that the *Nāṭyaśāstra* commences a long tradition of discourse on the nature of the aesthetic experience, the artistic content, form, process and response in the spectator and audience.

The *Nāṭyaśāstra* serves as an indispensable link between the realms of philosophy and aesthetics of mysticism and aesthetics. Discussions of a conceptual nature emerge from the seminal chapters VI and VII but each interpreter (more correctly, scholar-critic) takes into account other portions and chapters of the text. Also, discussions revolve around largely poetry and drama although the visual or representational arts are not excluded.

Abhinavagupta's influence on later scholarships on the *Nātyaśāstra* was profound and pervasive. He was acquainted with the works of predecessors, even the fine rhetoricians, Bhāmaha and Daṇḍin, also perhaps, Rājaśekhara. However, his influence on his followers is of great significance, Each succeeding writer may or may not have touched the source of the *Nāṭyaśāstra,* but had to encounter the mountain-peak of Abhinavagupta in constructing his theory of aesthetics or enunciating the structure of dramaturgy. This is as true of Sāgaranandin as of Rāmacandra or Bhoja, and, of course, Viśvanātha and Jagannātha.

While it would not be possible even to mention or summarize the varying positions of the successors of Abhinavagupta, it may be remembered that no succeeding writer, theoretician could ignore the discussions on the two crucial chapters of the *Nāṭyaśāstra,* namely, VI and VII on *rasa* and *bhāva,* and Abhinavagupta's commentary. It is also obvious that the commentary had reached all parts of India soon after its composition, although whether it was through oral discourse or through written texts, is a matter of debate and mystery.

Abhinava's near contemporaries and immediate successors, ranging from Dhanañjaya to Sāgaranandin, Rāmacandra to Bhoja, discreetly elaborate on these concepts. The tradition of discourse, both in dramaturgy as also poetics, continues until Viśvanātha and Jagannātha. The several streams and sub-streams again exemplify the phenomenon of continuity and change rather than 'static' repetition.

One can discern three principal trends in the 'successors' none of whom rises to the pinnacle of philosophic discourse of Abhinava. They are concerned with typologies of structure (e.g., Dhanañjaya's *Daśarūpaka*) or with the structure of drama *itivṛtta* as in the case of *Nāṭaka-lakṣaṇaratnakośa* and *Nāṭyadarpaṇa* or with the abstract content and form, *sthāyi bhāva, vyabhicāri bhāva* or their categories, such as, the long discussion by Bhoja in *Śṛṅgāra-prakāśa* or how these are to be depicted in drama or poetry. In poetics, from Kuntaka to Viśvanātha and Jagannātha, the echoes of Bharata and Abhinavagupta and an explicit referential dialogue is heard.

Obviously, it is neither possible nor necessary to trace this history of critical literature. Nevertheless, in mentioning them our purpose is only to point at the interwoven and multilayered character of these discussions.

Finally, in the fifteenth century appear the Goswamis, Rūpa and Jīva, as the exponents of Gauḍīya Vaiṣṇavism. *Rasa* as a concept again invites their attention. Just as they give a theological turn and interpretations to Jayadeva's *Gīta Govinda,* so also they extend the concept of '*rasa*', the experience of '*rasāsvāda* to the realm of devotion and *bhakti.* Abhinavagupta and others had extended/applied or implied philosophic school of thought to understanding and comprehending *rasa,* the Goswamis exemplify the reverse phenomenon where poetry (*kāvya*) and its characters (Rādha and Kṛṣna of the *Gīta Govinda*) and *rasa* of the *Nāṭyaśāstra* are systematically employed for the evolution of a full-fledged theory of *bhakti rasa.* The mutual interpenetration of fields is obvious. They enrich and deepen understanding.

Ujjvalnīlamaṇi and *Bhaktirasāmṛtasindhu* reveal an uncanny insight into the nature of the aesthetic experience, no doubt through the ecstasy of *surrender.* Common to both is the quality of transcendence of liberation and of release.

It is interesting to note that the fields of aesthetic and

philosophy were not mutually exclusive. Scholars have so far believed that aesthetics does not enter the Indian philosophic schools and systems. True as this is, the above discussion in respect of the Kashmiri commentators makes it clear that their position in the field of aesthetics perhaps emerged from or was inextricably linked to a particular philosophic school. So also is the popularly held notion of the divorce between theology, even religions, sects and theology and aesthetics. Here also the mutual interpenetration is clear and commands greater scholarship in-depth. Many more works of Śaiva Siddhānta and the Vaiṣṇava *āgamas* will reveal these interconnections. Indian art is not 'religious' in the ordinary sense, nor is there a theology of aesthetics but the two fields interpenetrate because they share the basic world-view in general and the specific goal of *mokṣa* and liberation, in particular. In the hierarchy of values, *mokṣa*, liberation, freedom from bondage, was the highest. The paths to attain this were varied, diversified and yet at certain moments, almost as confluences in a pilgrimage, they met, interacted and even interchanged places.

The *Nāṭyaśāstra* as a text, specially its chapters on *rasa* and *bhāva*, thus, serve as a vital 'bridge' of this interchange and interaction. The history of discourse makes this clear. Understandably, the effort to categorize these as philosophy, mysticism, religion, theology and secular art has been unsatisfying. Logically, it takes one to question the usual categories of sacred and secular art in the Indian context, religious and profane art, or between religion and art. The text of the *Nāṭyaśāstra* poses these questions to the modern reader who begins, alas, from a position of dichotomy and differentiation, polarity, and tension and is unable to see the whole. The *Nāṭyaśāstra*, on the other hand, starts from an integral vision, blossoms forth into a variegated manifestation of genres levels, schools and styles of an artistic presentation and aims to culminate through this orchestration to a repose, a state of equanimity of comprehension.

Scholars, readers of this text, also then have to be the initiated 'spectators' and readers of the text, *sahṛdaya* with *samavedana* (sympathy and empathy) if they are to relish, taste (*āsvāda*) this meal that Bharata lays out for the philosopher, theologian, literary critic and historian, dramatists, actor, dancer, musician and connoisseur, alike.

Conclusion

How can one conclude or come to a conclusion on the ever- flowing stream of the *Nāṭyaśāstra*? The 'text' is, as it were, the *gomukha* demarcating the glaciers above and the rivers which flow with the streams of the Alaknandā and the Mandākini, the Bhāgīrathi and others with their manifold confluences and some divergence but all of which we recognize as the Gaṅgā. The analogy of streams, confluences (*prayāga*) and the continuous flowing and yet changing nature of the river is the closest approximation by which the *paramparā* of the *Naṭyaśāstra*, the text and the dynamics of inflow confluences, outflow and ultimate inflows into the ocean, can be explained.

We began by addressing the question of authorship, period and location. A logical corollary was the related issue of the absolute or only relative importance of historicity, time in the Indian tradition. A re-reflection on these issues in the context of Bharata the author, and *Nāṭyaśāstra* the text, revealed that individual historical identity in terms of the physical event of birth and death or of information on personal life were not psychical concerns. Indeed these were almost irrelevant to the author in asserting his contribution in originating or developing a discourse. Instead, his concern was with situating himself in an ongoing discourse within a school of thought, the *paramparā*. Predecessors were important for locating the particular text against the contribution of not only those whom the author considered his peers but also those he identified as his contemporaries or possible successors. Thus the author's desire, his *uddeśya* (aim) and *saṅkalpa* (determination) to locate his work was a method of contextualizing the work in a system of thought and not in socio-historical terms. This is obvious in the case of the *Nāṭyaśāstra* as it is in respect of a very large body of creative and critical literature. The attitude of mind and the approach is shared by others and is evident in many texts of several disciplines and certainly those of the visual and the kinetic arts.

Once we began to look at the 'text' we confronted the fundamental question of the relationship of the oral and the written in the Indian tradition. The creation, whether in the field of what may be called revelation (*śruti*) and poetry (*kāvya*) or cognitive writing (here, *śāstra*), was primarily of the word 'articulated' rather than the 'word' written. Also, there was a sizeable gap between the date of composition of the text and even the earliest known written manuscripts of the text. A slightly deeper reflection made it clear that unlike the immutable *śruti*, here the written text could only at best be a close or the closest approximation to a faithful recording of the oral text, and also that the written text in the case of the *śāstra* could at best be a residual record or memory aid of a much deeper, more intense and pervasive oral discourse within the tradition. The *Nāṭyaśāstra* was no exception. The moment attention was focused on the nature of the transmission of the oral from master to disciple or from the preceptor of a school to the followers of a school and on the attempts to record the oral text as a written text, we confronted the real and complex issue of what constitutes an authentic text in the Indian tradition and what is the criterion of determining the authenticity of a text besides grammatical mistakes, scribe's errors. A consideration of this problem brought us face to face again with more complex issues of orality and methods of reconstructing or determining the authentic text at the stage of transcription. A highly systematized oral text once transcribed marked the beginning of other problems. Now the text travels to different parts of India, Nepal and Tibet through several centuries and is transcribed in different scripts. The determination of an authentic text on the basis of the different manuscripts is the puzzling and fascinating history of the *Nāṭyaśāstra*, as of many other texts. The search for more manuscripts and collation and editing of the diverse manuscripts to arrive at a definitive text is at this moment a continuing endeavour of two hundred years. No, one may say even eighteen hundred years.

It was with the hide and seek of the paths by which the stream of the textual tradition of the *Nāṭyaśāstra* flowed with the constant interplay of the oral and the written, the one language and many scripts, the one clear vision but many problematic boulders of determining an authentic and definitive text, that we realized that within the tradition the course of the river, the process, was more important than the frozen, fixed, sealed entity of a text at a particular moment.

The quest for identifying the course of the river naturally led us to the perennial snows of the world view and conceptual thought of the Indian tradition. We thus paused to look at the world view which influenced if not determined the text of the *Nāṭyaśāstra*. This was the inspiration of the *Nāṭyaśāstra* as also its larger context. Soon we observed that the *Nāṭyaśāstra* brought into one fold the cosmology of the Vedas, the speculative thought of the Upaniṣads and the structure of the rituals of the Brāhmaṇas as also the state of knowledge in the disciplines of astronomy, mathematics, medicine. The employment of the two referential terms *yoga* and *yajña* were contextually loaded. Employment of these terms in the realm of aesthetics was of great significance. The identification of the perennial sources also enabled us to look at the implicit and explicit levels of the text. The *Nāṭyaśāstra* employed the metaphor of the seed (*bīja*) and the tree, the process of sprouting, blooming and decay and renewal, throughout, to comprehend the nature of the aesthetic universe. It was an organism; the process was primary. The metaphor of body (*śarīra*) and the soul (*ātman*) were terms of structure used to explain the formal values of a piece of art. Throughout, the text moved from process to structure and the two were intertwined. Important was the author's commitment to the notion of unmanifest and manifest, *avyakta* and *vyakta,* and therefore the repetitive reference to the secret (*guha*) but very real origins of creativity as in the womb (*garbha*) and all that it denotes in a long history of discourse in all disciplines. It is symbolically concretized as the *garbha gṛha* in Indian architecture. The text at the explicit level was thus a framework for comprehending the more complex dynamics of concurrency and simultaneity rather than sequentiality. Our analysis, however brief, perhaps made it clear that the text was neither a compilation nor an aggregation. It emerged from a single integral vision and with purpose and design was assimilative of many discipline ranging from cosmology, mythology, mathematics and medicine, and was multi-layered. It moved concurrently at the level of the physical and the metaphysical, the terrestrial and the celestial, the purely biological and the psychical, the sensuous and the spiritual.

The structure was based on the well chiselled system of the triads (*traya*) of the planes of living and the orders of space and time and the gradations of the gross and subtle. The whole spectrum of the life phenomenon in all its horizontal and vertical dimensions was comprehended.

Further, it became evident that the *Nāṭyaśāstra* with great dexterity lays down the tools and instrumentalities by which the world of the imagination can be conjured. The author's intention is neither imitation as replication nor historical re-narration. The closest approximation in modern-day vocabulary would be creative simulation and presentation of a programme of 'virtual reality'. Perhaps modern technology provides a clue to understanding the crucial words *anukaraṇa, anukīrtana* and *anuvyavasāya* in the *Nāṭyaśāstra.* We have not dwelt at length on a discussion of the content of each of the chapters of the *Nāṭyaśāstra;* we have confined ourselves to laying bare the structural frame of the *Nāṭyaśāstra.* The core concepts such as *anukaraṇa* and *anukīrtana* have come up for discussion while discussing the interpreters of Bharata. This discussion assumes importance in the light of the contemporary discussion on the nature of phenomenon and its mirrorizing and imaging in creation. The *Nāṭyaśāstra* as confluence, with its concurrent dimensions and levels of meaning and latent capacity for multi-interpretations and inbuilt rigorous flexibility, became the fountainhead and source for other simultaneously running streams. The two processes of concurrency and simultaneity were in evidence. We identified two. One, of the textual tradition of the different arts which were inspired and effected by the *Nāṭyaśāstra* especially in *saṅgīta, nāṭya, vāstu, śilpa* and *sāhitya* and the other of the interpreters normally called commentators. Amongst the many texts of the first stream we have been obliged to exclude altogether here the sections of the Purāṇas from *Agni* to the *Viṣṇudharmottara* to *Vāyu* and *Matsya* and others altogether, as it would not have been correct to do so without undertaking a fresh investigation into the relationship of *Purāṇa* and *Śāstra.* So also in the case of the second stream (that is, interpreters). A very selective discussion has been attempted of a few interpreters and their positions only in relation to the key concepts of the *Nāṭyaśāstra* and not their entire writing. Thus even a brief presentation of the schools of poetics of Bhāmaha, Vāmana and Daṇḍin as also *Dhvani* (Ānandavardhana) had to be excluded.

Throughout the attempt was to carefully follow the course of the river and streams of the *Nāṭyaśāstra*, notwithstanding the other equally valid and related rivers of the tradition even in the field of aesthetics, especially poetics (*alaṁkāra*). Our examination, however brief as a bird's eye-view, made it clear that the text came into being from the perennial well-spring of the eternal snows of thought, was nourished and nurtured by related disciplines, and in turn gave birth to other texts not only in the specific but all comprehensive category of *nāṭya* but also in others which were subsumed in *nāṭya,* e.g. *nṛtta, saṅgīta, kāvya, sāhitya, śilpa,* etc. Alongside was the concurrent phenomenon of the interpretation through the application of the tenets of diverse schools of philosophy. Multiple theoretical positions were taken to interpret the text. The interface of aesthetics and theology and even religion was evident in the commentators of the post-sixteenth century. And finally the text was examined as a source for creativity, for in its final analysis art is a matter of experience, undifferentiated in a state of release, and the expressions are the outer manifestations, all serving as bridges of communication to evoke a similar and analogous state of being in the spectator and receiver. The importance of the

Nāṭyaśāstra and its interpreters as fore-runners of the theories of communication, reception, empathy was perhaps clear. Bharata was after all primarily and fundamentally revealing the epistemology of experience and of expression and communication, in short, *prayoga.*

The history of discourse comes full circle, except (as has been stated in the introduction) that the discussion would not be complete without re-viewing the critical discourse of the last century and a half. That too had to be excluded because now the interpreters and the critical writers no longer belonged to the same landscapes, mental and physical. We would have to go into the background and conditioning of the observer (the Orientalist and the Modernist) before identifying what he observed in the text of the *Nāṭyaśāstra.* Discontinuity, assertion of the individual position, would be the key words and that would be and is another journey for another time.

Bibliography

Abhinavagupta. *Īśvarapratyabhijñāvivṛtivimarśinī,* edited by M. Kauḷ Sastri, K.S.T.S. LXV, Department of Research and Publication, Jammu & Kashmir State, Srinagar, 1943.

Agrawala, V.S. *India as Known to Pāṇini,* Lucknow University, Lucknow, 1953.

———. *Sparks from the Vedic Fire,* School of Vedic Studies, Varanasi, 1962.

Ahobala. *Saṅgīta Pārijāta,* Calcutta and Hathras.

Barth, Auguste (review of Regnaud, 1880, 1881). *Revue critique d'histoire et de litterature,* reprinted in *Oeuvres de Auguste Barth,* Vol. 3, Leroux, Paris, 1917.

———. (review of Grosset, 1888). *Revue critique d'histoire et de litterature,* reprinted in *Oeuvres de Auguste Barth,* Vol. 3, Leroux, Paris, 1917.

Bhāmaha. *Kāvyālaṃkāra,* edited by B.N. Sarma and B. Upadhyaya, *Chowkhambha Sanskrit series,* Varanasi.

Bhartṛhari. *Vākyapadīya,* Kāṇḍa 1, edited with the *Vṛtti* and *Paddhati* commentary of Vṛṣabhadeva by K.A. Subrahmanya Iyer, *Deccan College Monograph series,* Poona, 1966.

Breloer, Bernhard. *Die Grundelemente der altindischen Musik nach dem Bhāratīya-nātya-śāstra,* Text. Übersetzung und Erklärung, Bonn, 1922.

Byrski, M.C. *Concept of Ancient Indian Theatre,* Munshiram Manoharlal, Delhi, 1974.

Chakravarti, H.N. 'Bīja', in the *Kalātattvakośa* volume, edited by Bettina Bäumer, Indira Gandhi National Centre for the Arts and Motilal Banarsidass, Delhi, 1988.

Chandra, Pramod. *Studies in Indian Temple Architecture,* Calcutta University, Calcutta, 1975.

Chandrasekharan, K. and V.H. Subrahmanya Sastri. *Sanskrit Literature,* The P.E.N. All India Centre, Bombay, 1951.

Coomaraswamy and Duggirala. *Mirror of Gesture*; two different recensions have been used by each of the editors, Munshiram Manoharlal, Delhi, 1970.

Dallapicolla, A. *Śāstric Traditions in Indian Arts,* Vols. I and II, Steiner Verlag, Wiesbaden, 1989, 'Introduction' and specially the following articles: Kapila Vatsyayan, 'Inaugural Address'; T.S. Maxwell, 'Śilpa versus Śāstra'; Sheldon Pollock, 'Idea of Śāstra in Traditional India'; D.H.H. Ingalls, *Dhvanyāloka*; Harvard University Press, Cambridge, MA, 1990.

Daṇḍin. *Kāvyādarśa,* edited by N. Sastri, 1980.

Danielou, A. *Introduction to the Study of Musical Scales,* Oriental Books, New Delhi, 1979 (reprint).

Dasgupta, S.N. *A History of Indian Philosophy,* Cambridge, 1957.

Dasgupta, S.N. and S.K. De. *A History of Sanskrit Literature,* University of Calcutta, Calcutta, 1962.

De, S.K. 'The Bhakti-Rasa-Śāstra of Bengal Vaiṣṇavism', *Indian Historical Quarterly,* Vol. 8, 1932.

———. 'The Theory of *Rasa* in Sanskrit Poetics', *Sir Asutosh Mookerjee Silver Jubilee Volume III,* Orientalia, Part II, 1922.

———. *A History of Sanskrit Literature*, University of Calcutta, Calcutta, 1947.

———. *Aspects of Sanskrit Literature*, Firma K.L. Mukhopadhyay, Calcutta, 1959 (reprints of nine essays).

———. *History of Sanskrit Poetics*, second edition, Firma K.L. Mukhopadhyay, Calcutta, 1960.

Dhaky, M.A. and Michael Meister. *Encyclopaedia of Indian Temple Architecture*, Vol. 2, Part IV, Calcutta University Press, Calcutta, 1983.

Dhanañjaya. *Daśarūpaka*: (i) with the commentary of Dhanika, Nirnayasagar Press, fifth edition; (ii) with Dhanika's *Avaloka* and Pt Sudarsana's *Prabhā*, Gujarati Printing Press, Bombay, 1927; (iii) with Dhanika's *Avaloka* and the sub-commentary *Laghuṭīkā* by Bhaa-Narasiṁha, edited with Introduction and Notes by T. Venkatacharya, Adyar Library and Research Centre, Adyar, 1968; (iv) Text, English translation, Notes, etc, by George C.O. Haas, Columbia University, edited in 1912, Indian edition by Motilal Banarsidass, 1966.

Dhruva, H.H. 'Bharata Nāṭya Śāstra; or, the Indian Dramatics by Bharata Muni', *The Imperial and Asiatic Quarterly Review and Oriental and Colonial Record, Third series*, Vol. 2, 1896.

Eggeling, J. *The Śatapatha Brāhmaṇa*, translation in the *Sacred Books of the East series*, Vols. XII, XXVI, XLI, XLIII, XLIV, Motilal Banarasidass, Delhi, 1978.

Feistel, Harmut-Ortwin. 'The Pūrvaraṅga and the Chronology of the Pre-Classical Sanskrit Theatre', in *Sanskrit Ranga*, Annual VI, Madras, 1972.

Ghosh, Manomohan, 'Prākṛta Verses in the Bharata-Nāṭyaśāstra', supplement to *Indian Historical Quarterly*, No. 8, 1932.

Ghosal, S.N. *The Inception of the Sanskrit Drama*, Calcutta Book House, Calcutta, 1977.

Gnoli, R. *The Aesthetic Experience according to Abhinavagupta*, Serie Orientale Roma XI, ISEMO, Roma, 1956.

Grosset, Joanny. *Contributions a l'etude de la musique hindoue*, extract from Bibliotheque de la Faculte des Lettres de Lyon, 1888.

———. *Bharatiya-nātya-cāśtram: Traite de Bharata sur le theatre.* Texte Sanskrit, Paris, 1898.

Gupta, C.B. *The Indian Theatre*, Motilal Banarsidass, Banaras, 1954.

Hall, Fitz-Edward. *The Daśa-rūpa, or Hindu Canons of Dramaturgy by Dhananjaya, with the exposition of Dhanika, the Avaloka,* The Royal Asiatic Society, Calcutta, 1865.

Heymann, Wilhelm. 'Über Bharata's Nāṭyaśāstram', in *Nachrichten von der königlichen Gesellschaft der Wissenschaften*, Goetingen, 1874.

Hillebrandt, A. *Ritual Literature*, Strassburg, 1897.

———. *Über die Anjanga des Indischen Dramas*, Munich, 1914.

Hiriyanna, M. 'Indian Aesthetics', in *Proceedings and Transactions of the First Oriental Conference*, Bhandarkar Oriental Research Institute, Poona, 1922.

Hume, Robert Ernest. *The Thirteen Principal Upaniṣads*, translated from the Sanskrit, Oxford University Press, 1931 (second revised edition).

Ingalls, D.H.H. *An Anthology of Sanskrit Court Poetry*, H.O.S. No. 44, a translation of the *Subhāṣitaratnakośa*, Cambridge, MA, 1965.

———. *The Dhvanyāloka of Ānandavardhana with the Locana of Abhinavagupta*, Harvard University Press, Cambridge, MA, 1990.

Kane, P.V. 'Gleanings from the Abhinavabhāratī', *Pathak Commemoration Volume*, BORI, Poona, 1934.

———. *History of Sanskrit Poetics*, Nirnayasagar Press, Bombay, 1931.

Kale, Pramod. *The Theatric Universe*, Popular Prakashan, Bombay, 1974.

Keith, A.B. (ed. and trans.). *The Aitareya Āraṇyaka*, Clarendon Press, Oxford, 1909.

———. *Classical Sanskrit Literature*, YMCA, Delhi, 1966.

———. *The Sanskrit Drama*, Oxford University Press, 1924.

Konow, Sten. *Das Ind Drama*, Berlin and Leipzig, 1920.

Kramrisch, Stella. *The Hindu Temple*, University of Calcutta, Calcutta, 1946 and Motilal Banarsidass, Delhi, 1991.

———. 'The Temple as Puruṣa', in *Studies in Indian Temple Architecture*, Calcutta University Press, Calcutta, 1975.

Krishnamoorthy, K. *The Dhvanyāloka and its Critics*, Kāvyālaya Publishers, Mysore, 1968.

———. *Essays in Sanskrit Criticism*, Karnataka University, Dharwar, 1964.

Kuiper, F.B.J. *Varuṇa and Vidūṣaka*, North Holland Publishing Company, Amsterdam, 1977.

Kulkarni, K.P. *Sanskrit Drama and Dramatists*, Satara City, 1927.

Lath, Mukund. *Dattilam*, Impex, Delhi, 1978; Indira Gandhi National Centre for the Arts and Motilal Banarsidass, Delhi, 1988.

Lévi, Sylvain. *Le Theatre Indien*, Emile Bouillon, Librairie Editeur, Paris, 1890; new edition with introduction by Louis Renou, College de France, Paris, 1963.

———. *Rapport de M. Sylvain Lévi . . . sur sa mission dans l'Inde et au Japon*, Comptes Rendus de l'Academie des Inscriptions et Belles Lettres 4e serie, tome 27, 1899.

Lidova, Natalia. *Drama and Ritual of Early Hinduism*, Motilal Banarsidass, Delhi, 1994.

Lüders, H. *Philologica Indica*, Göttingen, 1940.

Macdonell, A.A. *History of Sanskrit Literature*, Munshiram Manoharlal, Delhi, 1962.

Mankad, D.R. *The Types of Sanskrit Drama*, Urmi Prakashan Mandir, Denso Hall, Karachi, 1936.

Mataṅga. *Bṛhaddeśī*, edited by Premlata Sharma, Vol. I, Indira Gandhi National Centre for the Arts and Motilal Banarsidass, Delhi, 1992.

Masson, J.L. and M.V. Patwardhan. *Śāntarasa and Abhinavagupta's Philosophy of Aesthetics*, BORI, Poona, 1969.

———. *Aesthetic Rapture: The Rasādhyāya of the Nāṭyaśāstra*, 2 vols., Deccan College, Poona, 1970.

Miller, C.J. 'Bharata and the Authorship and Age of the Nāṭya Śāstra', in *Sanskrit Ranga*, Annual VI, Madras, 1972.

Misra, V.N. and P.L. Sharma. 'Lōka', in *Kalātattvakośa*, Vol. II, Indira Gandhi National Centre for the Arts and Motilal Banarsidass, Delhi, 1992.

Nandikeśvara. *Abhinayadarpaṇa*, edited by Manomohan Ghosh, *Sanskrit series*, Calcutta, 1934.

Nāṭyaśāstra: A Treatise on Ancient Indian Dramaturgy and Histrionics, ascribed to Bharatamuni, Sanskrit text and English translation, edited by Manomohan Ghosh, Vols. I and II, Asiatic Society, Calcutta, 1951.

Nāṭyaśāstra, Vol. II, text, edited by Manomohan Ghosh, Bibliotheca Indica, The Asiatic Society, Calcutta, 1956.

Nāṭyaśāstra: Contributions to the History of the Hindu Drama, edited by Manomohan Ghosh, Firma K.L. Mukhopadhyay, Calcutta, 1958.

Nāṭyaśāstra, edited by Manomohan Ghosh, Vol. II, translation, Bibliotheca Indica, The Asiatic Society, Calcutta, 1961.

Nāṭyaśāstra, edited by Manomohan Ghosh, Vol. I, Manisha Granthalaya, Calcutta, 1967.

Nāṭyaśāstra, edited by Manomohan Ghosh, translation:.Vol. I, revised second edition, Manisha Granthalaya, Calcutta, 1967.

Nāṭyaśāstra, with the commentary of Abhinavagupta, edited by M.R. Kavi, *Gaekwad Oriental series,* Baroda, 1926.

Nāṭyaśāstra, edited with an introduction and index by M.R. Kavi, Vol. II, *Gaekwad Oriental series,* Baroda, 1934.

Nāṭyaśāstra, Vol. III, edited with an index by M.R. Kavi, *Gaekwad Oriental series,* Baroda, 1954.

Nāṭyaśāstra of Bharatamuni, with the commentary by Abhinavagupta, edited by M.R. Kavi, Vol. I, *Gaekwad Oriental series,* Baroda, 1956.

Nāṭyaśāstra, Vol. IV, edited by M.R. Kavi, *Gaekwad Oriental series,* Baroda, 1964.

Nāṭyaśāstra of Bharatamuni, edited by Sivadatta and Kasinath Pandurang Parab, *Kāvyamāla* 42, Nirnayasagar Press, Bombay, 1894.

Paṇḍarīka, Viṭṭhala. *Nartananirṇaya,* edited by Mandakranta Bose, General Printers and Publishers, Calcutta, 1991.

———. *Nartananirṇaya,* edited by R. Sathyanarayana, Indira Gandhi National Centre for the Arts and Motilal Banarsidass, New Delhi, 1994.

Pandey, K.C. *Comparative Aesthetics,* Vols. I and II, Chowkhamba, Varanasi, 1959.

———. *Abhinavagupta, An Historical and Philosophical Study,* Chowkhamba, Varanasai, 1966 (second edition).

Pischel, Richard (review of Regnaud 1884). *Gottingische Gelehrte Anzeigen,* 1885.

Raghavan, V. 'The Vṛttis', *Journal of the Oriental Research,* Madras, 1932.

——— 'A Note on the Name Daśarūpaka', in *Journal of Oriental Research,*Vol. III, Madras, 1932.

———. 'The Concept of Lakṣaṇa in Bharata', in *Journal of the Oriental Research,* Vol. VI, Madras, 1932.

———. *The Number of Rasas,* second edition, Adyar Library and Research Centre, Madras, 1967.

———. *Some Concepts of the Alaṁkāraśāstra,* Adyar Library and Research Centre, Madras, 1942.

———. 'Nāṭyadharmī and Lokadharmī', in *Journal of Oriental Research,* Vol. VII, 1933, Vol. VIII, 1934, Madras.

———. *Sanskrit Drama, Its Aesthetics and Production,* 1993.

——— (ed.). *Nṛttīratnāvali of Jayasenāpati, Government Oriental series,* Government Oriental Manuscripts Library, Madras, 1965.

——— (ed.). *Bhoja's Śṛṅgāra Prakāśa,* Punarvasu, Madras, 1963.

Raghavan, V. and Nagendra. *An Introduction to Indian Poetics,* Macmillan, Madras, 1970.

Rājaśekhara. *Karpūramañjari,* edited and translated by Sten Konow, Harvard University, Cambridge, MA, 1901.

Rāmacandra and Guṇacandra. *Nāṭyadarpaṇa*: (i) edited with Introduction in English and Indices by G.K. Shrigondekar, *Gaekwad Oriental series,* No. 48, Oriental Institute, Baroda, 1929; (ii) Hindi *Nāṭyadarpaṇa* by Acharya Vishveshvara, Hindi Vibhaga, Delhi University, Delhi, 1961; (iii) a study by K.H. Trivedi, L.D. Institute of Indology, Ahmedabad, 1966.

Sāgaranandin. *Nāṭaka-lakṣaṇa-ratṇakośa* (i) edited by Miles Dilon, Oxford University Press, London, 1937 (Vol. 1, text); (ii) translated into English by Miles Dilon, Murray Fowler and V. Raghavan, Introduction and Notes by V. Raghvan, *Transactions of the American Philosophical Society,* New series, Vol. 50, Part 9, American Philosophical Society, Philadelphia, 1960; (iii) with

Hindi commentary *Prabhā* by Babulal Shukla Shastri, Chowkhambha Sanskrit Series Office, Varanasi, 1972.

Śāradātanaya. *Bhāvaprakāśana*, edited by K.S. Ramaswamy, *Gaekwad Oriental series*, No. 14, Baroda, 1930.

———. *Bhāvaprakāśana*, edited with Introduction and Indices by Yadugiri Yatiraja Swami and K.S. Ramaswami Shastri, *Gaekwad Oreintal series*, No. 45, Oriental Institute, Baroda, 1968.

Saraswati Amma. *Geometry in Ancient and Medieval India*, Motilal Banarsidass, New Delhi, 1979.

Sarkar, H. *The Monuments of Kerala*, Archaeological Survey of India, New Delhi, 1973.

Sankaran, S. *Some Aspects of Literary Criticism in Sanskrit or the Theories of Rasa and Dhvani*, University of Madras, 1929.

Śārṅgadeva. *Saṅgītaratnākara*, edited by R.K. Shringy, The Adyar Library and Research Centre of the Theosophical Society, Madras, 1943.

———. *Saṅgītaratnākara*, edited by S. Subrahmanya Sastri with Kalānidhi of Kallināth and Sudhākara of Siṁhabhūpāla, Vol. IV, Adhyāya 7, The Adyar Library and Research Centre of the Theosophical Society, Adyar, Madras, 1953.

Sharma, B.N. and B. Upadhyaya. *The Nāṭyaśāstra of Bharata, Kashi Sanskrit series*, Chowkhambha Sanskrit Series Office, Varanasi, 1929.

Shastri, Haraprasad. 'The Origin of Indian Drama', *JPASB*, Vol. V, Calcutta, 1909.

Shastri, S.N. *The Laws and Practice of Sanskrit Drama*, Chowkhamba Sanskrit Studies, Vol. XIV, Varanasi, 1961.

Shekhar, I. *Sanskrit Drama: Its Origin and Decline*, E.J. Brill, Leiden, Netherlands, 1960.

Śilpaprakāśa, edited by Alice Boner, E.J. Brill, Leiden, Netherlands, 1966.

Somnath. *Rāga-vibōdha*, Lahore, 1910.

Swami Prajnanananda. *A History of Indian Music*, Vol. I, Ramakrishna Vedanta Math, Calcutta, 1963.

Tripathi, K.D. 'Lakṣaṇa', in *Kalātattvakośa*, edited by Bettina Bäumer, Vol. I, Indira Gandhi National Centre for the Arts and Motilal Banarsidass, Delhi, 1988.

Upadhyaya, Baldeva. *Saṁskṛta Sāhitya kā Itihāsa* (Hindi), Sharada Mandir, Varanasi.

Vāmana. *Kāvyālaṁkāra*, edited by K.P. Parab and W Pansikar, Bombay, 1926.

Vatsyayan, Kapila. *The Square and the Circle of the Indian Arts*, Roli Books International, New Delhi, 1983.

———. 'Mārga and Deśa' and 'Naṭya and Lokadharmī', in the *Ludwik Sternbach Memorial Lecture*, Vol. I, Akhil Bharatiya Sanskrit Parishad, Lucknow, 1979.

———. 'Indian Art—The One and the Many', Nehru Memorial Lecture, London, 1993.

———. *Classical Indian Dance in Literature and the Arts*, Sangeet Natak Akademi, New Delhi, 1977 (second edition).

———. 'Vāstupurusa Maṇḍala', *Vistāra*, Festival of India, 1986.

———. 'The Flying Messenger', *Kalakshetra Bulletin*, Adyar.

———. *The Karaṇas of the Temple of Śārṅgapāṇi*, Society for Archaeological Historical and Epigraphical Research, Madras, 1982.

———. 'The Dance Sculptures of the Lora-Djonggrang (Prambanam)', *NCPA Journal*, Vol. VI, No. I, Bombay, March 1977.

———. *Mewāri Gīta Govinda*, National Museum, New Delhi 1987.

———. *Dance in Indian Painting*, Abhinava Prakashan, Delhi, 1982, Chapter II on Rajasthani paintings.

———. *Traditional Indian Theatre: Multiple Streams*, National Book Trust, New Delhi, 1981.

Viśvanātha. *Sāhityadarpaṇa*, edited by Ramacharana Tarkavagisa Bhattacharya, with the commentary *Vivṛti* and *Vivṛtipūrti* of Durgaprasad Dwivedi by Srinivasa Venkatarama, Nirnayasagar Press, Bombay, 1915.

Wright, J.C. *Vṛtti on the Daśarūpakavidhānādhyāya of the Abhinavabhāratī, A study of the history of the text of the Nāṭyaśāstra*, B.S.O.A.S., Vol. XXVI, Part I, London, 1963.

Zimmer, H. *Philosophies of India*, Bollingen Foundation, New York, 1951.

Appendix: Database of *Nāṭyaśāstra**

Serial No. 1

Title Proper	Nāṭyaśāstra
Author	Bharata Muni
Institution	L.D. Institute, Ahmedabad
Library Accession No.	4459
Language	Sanskrit
Script	Devanagari
Collection	Muni Puṇyavijaya Collection

Serial No. 2

Title Proper	Nāṭyaśāstra
Author	Bharata Muni
Institution	L.D. Institute, Ahmedabad
Library Accession No.	11019
Language	Sanskrit
Script	Devanagari

Serial No. 3

Title Proper	Nāṭyaśāstra

* Database of manuscripts compiled in the Indira Gandhi National Centre for the Arts. Copyright owner: Indira Gandhi National Centre for the Arts, New Delhi. I am indebted to my colleagues in IGNCA for having evolved this Database. I would like to thank specially Dr N.D. Sharma for having finalized this compilation.

Author	Bharata Muni
Institution	Nepalese Libraries at Kathmandu
Library Accession No.	8
Language	Sanskrit

Serial No. 4

Title Proper	Nāṭyaśāstra
Author	Bharata Muni
Institution	Calicut University Library, Calicut
Accession No.	302
Language	Sanskrit
Script	Grantha

Serial No. 5

Title Proper	Nāṭyaśāstra
Author	Bharata Muni
Institution	Kurukshetra University, Kurukshetra
Library Accession No.	H. 50611 (S.No. 488)
Language	Sanskrit
Script	Devanagari

Serial No. 6

Title Proper	Nāṭyaśāstra
Author	Bharata Muni
Institution	Maharaja Sawai Mansingh II Museum, Jaipur
Library Accession No.	6587
Language	Sanskrit
Script	Devanagari

Serial No. 7

Title Proper	Nāṭyaśāstra
Author	Bharata Muni
Institution	Maharaja Sawai Mansingh II Museum, Jaipur

Library Accession No.	6646
Language	Sanskrit
Script	Devanagari

Serial No. 8

Title Proper	Nāṭyaśāstra
Author	Bharata Muni
Institution	Sawai Mansingh Museum II, Pothikhana of Jaipur, Jaipur
Library Accession No.	6882
Language	Sanskrit

Serial No. 9

Title Proper	Nāṭyaśāstra
Author	Bharata Muni
Institution	Maharaja Sawai Mansingh II Museum, Jaipur
Library Accession No.	7556
Language	Sanskrit
Script	Devanagari

Serial No. 10

Title Proper	Nāṭyaśāstra
Author	Bharata Muni
Institution	Thanjavur Maharaja Serfoji's Saraswati Mahal Library, Thanjavur
Library Accession No.	10650
Language	Sanskrit
Script	Telugu

Serial No. 11

Title Proper	Nāṭyaśāstra
Author	Bharata Muni
Institution	Thanjavur Maharaja Serfoji's Saraswati Mahal Library, Thanjavur

Library Accession No.	10651
Language	Sanskrit
Script	Telugu

Serial No. 12

Title Proper	Nāṭyaśāstra
Author	Bharata Muni
Institution	Thanjavur Maharaja Serfoji's Saraswati Mahal Library, Thanjavur
Library Accession No.	10652
Language	Sanskrit
Script	Telugu

Serial No. 13

Title Proper	Nāṭyaśāstra
Author	Bharata Muni
Institution	Shri R.V. Govt. College Library, Tripunithura
Library Accession No.	C–11
Language	Sanskrit
Script	Malayalam

Serial No. 14

Title Proper	Nāṭyaśāstra with Abhinavabhāratī
Author	Bharata Muni
Commentator	Abhinavagupta
Institution	Shri R.V. Govt. College Library, Tripunithura
Library Accession No.	60–A
Language	Sanskrit
Script	Malayalam

Serial No. 15

Title Proper	Nāṭyaśāstra
Author	Bharata Muni

Institution	Sh. Venkateshvara Oriental Research Institute, Tirupati
Library Accession No.	PL-329
Language	Sanskrit
Script	Telugu

Serial No. 16

Title Proper	Nāṭyaśāstra with commentary
Author	Bharata Muni
Commentator	Mānyapati
Institution	Sh. Venkateshvara Oriental Research Institute, Tirupati
Library Accession No.	P. 7107
Language	Sanskrit
Script	Devanagari

Serial No. 17

Title Proper	Nāṭyaśāstra
Author	Bharata Muni
Institution	Sh. Venkateshvara Oriental Research Institute, Tirupati
Library Accession No.	P. 7562A
Language	Sanskrit
Script	Devanagari

Serial No. 18

Title Proper	Nāṭyaśāstra
Author	Bharata Muni
Institution	Sh. Venkateshvara Oriental Research Institute, Tirupati
Library Accession No.	PL-7599-B
Language	Sanskrit
Script	Telugu

Serial No. 19

Title Proper	Nāṭyaśāstra
Author	Bharata Muni
Institution	Sh. Venkateshvara Oriental Research Institute, Tirupati
Library Accession No.	P-7617-B
Language	Sanskrit
Script	Telugu

Serial No. 20

Title Proper	Nāṭyaśāstra
Author	Bharata Muni
Institution	Curator's Office Library, Trivandrum
Library Accession No.	68
Language	Sanskrit

Serial No. 21

Title Proper	Nāṭyaśāstra
Author	Bharata Muni
Institution	Curator's Office Library, Trivandrum
Library Accession No.	89
Language	Sanskrit

Serial No. 22

Title Proper	Nāṭyaśāstra with Abhinavabhāratī
Author	Bharata Muni
Commentator	Abhinavagupta
Institution	University Manuscripts Library, Trivandrum
Library Accession No.	126
Language	Sanskrit

Serial No. 23

Title Proper	Abhinavabhāratī

Commentator	Abbhinavagupta
Institution	Curator's Office Library, Trivandrum
Library Accession No.	137
Language	Sanskrit

Serial No. 24

Title Proper	Abhinavabhāratī
Commentator	Abhinavagupta
Institution	Curator's Office Library, Trivandrum
Library Accession No.	138
Language	Sanskrit

Serial No. 25

Title Proper	Abhinavabhāratī
Commentator	Abhinavagupta
Institution	Curator's Office Library, Trivandrum
Library Accession No.	139
Language	Sanskrit

Serial No. 26

Title Proper	Nāṭyaśāstra
Author	Bharata Muni
Institution	Curator's Office Library, Trivandrum
Library Accession No.	141
Language	Sanskrit

Serial No. 27

Title Proper	Nāṭyaśāstra with Abhinavabhāratī
Author	Bharata Muni
Commentator	Abhinavagupta
Institution	University Manuscripts Library, Trivandrum
Library Accession No.	216-A
Language	Sanskrit

Serial No. 28

Title Proper	Nāṭyaśāstra with Abhinavabhāratī
Author	Bharata Muni
Commentator	Abhinavagupta
Institution	University Manuscripts Library, Trivandrum
Library Accession No.	216-B
Language	Sanskrit

Serial No. 29

Title Proper	Nāṭyaśāstra with Abhinavabhāratī
Author	Bharata Muni
Commentator	Abhinavagupta
Institution	University Manuscripts Library, Trivandrum
Library Accession No.	216-C
Language	Sanskrit

Serial No. 30

Title Proper	Nāṭyaśāstra with Nāṭyavedavivṛtti
Author	Bharata Muni
Commentator	Abhinavagupta
Institution	University Manuscripts Library, Trivandrum
Library Accession No.	T. 259
Language	Sanskrit
Script	Devanagari

Serial No. 31

Title Proper	Nāṭyaveda with commentary
Author	Bharata Muni
Institution	University Manuscripts Library, Trivandrum
Library Accession No.	289

Language	Sanskrit
Script	Malayalam

Serial No. 32

Title Proper	Nāṭyaśāstra and Abhinavabhāratī
Author	Bharata Muni
Commentator	Abhinavagupta
Institution	University Manuscripts Library, Trivandrum
Library Accession No.	T-551
Language	Sanskrit
Script	Devanagari

Serial No. 33

Title Proper	Nāṭyavedavivṛtti
Commentator	Abhinavagupta
Institution	University Manuscripts Library, Trivandrum
Library Accession No.	T-551 A
Language	Sanskrit
Script	Devanagari

Serial No. 34

Title Proper	Nāṭyavedavivṛtti
Commentator	Abhinavagupta
Institution	University Manuscripts Library, Trivandrum
Library Accession No.	T-551 B
Language	Sanskrit
Script	Devanagari

Serial No. 35

Title Proper	Nāṭyavedavivṛtti
Commentator	Abhinavagupta

Institution	University Manuscripts Library, Trivandrum
Library Accession No.	T-551 C
Language	Sanskrit
Script	Devanagari

Serial No. 36

Title Proper	Nāṭyaśāstra with Abhinavabhāratī
Author	Bharata Muni
Commentator	Abhinavagupta
Institution	University Manuscripts Library, Trivandrum
Library Accession No.	T. 566-A
Language	Sanskrit
Script	Devanagari

Serial No. 37

Title Proper	Nāṭyaśāstra with Abhinavabhāratī
Author	Bharata Muni
Commentator	Abhinavagupta
Institution	University Manuscripts Library, Trivandrum
Library Accession No.	T. 566-B
Language	Sanskrit
Script	Devanagari

Serial No. 38

Title Proper	Nāṭyaśāstra with Abhinavabhāratī
Author	Bharata Muni
Commentator	Abhinavagupta
Institution	University Manuscripts Library, Trivandrum
Library Accession No.	T. 566-C
Language	Sanskrit
Script	Devanagari

Serial No. 39

Title Proper	Nāṭyaśāstra with Abhinavabhāratī
Author	Bharata Muni
Commentator	Abhinavagupta
Institution	University Manuscripts Library, Trivandrum
Library Accession No.	1217
Language	Sanskrit

Serial No. 40

Title Proper	Nāṭyaśāstra with Abhinavabhāratī
Author	Bharata Muni
Commentator	Abhinavagupta
Institution	University Manuscripts Library, Trivandrum
Library Accession No.	1218
Language	Sanskrit

Serial No. 41

Title Proper	Nāṭyaśāstra with Abhinavabhāratī
Author	Bharata Muni
Commentator	Abhinavagupta
Institution	University Manuscripts Library, Trivandrum
Library Accession No.	1219
Language	Sanskrit

Serial No. 42

Title Proper	Nāṭyaśāstra with Abhinavabhāratī
Author	Bharata Muni
Commentator	Abhinavagupta
Institution	University Manuscripts Library, Trivandrum
Library Accession No.	1404
Language	Sanskrit

Serial No. 43

Title Proper	Nāṭyaśāstra
Author	Bharata Muni
Institution	University Manuscripts Library, Trivandrum
Library Accession No.	C-1809-C
Language	Sanskrit
Script	Malayalam

Serial No. 44

Title Proper	Nāṭyaśāstra with Abhinavabhāratī
Author	Bharata Muni
Commentator	Abhinavagupta
Institution	University Manuscripts Library, Trivandrum
Library Accession No.	C-1854
Language	Sanskrit
Script	Malayalam

Serial No. 45

Title Proper	Nāṭyaśāstra
Author	Bharata Muni
Institution	University Manuscripts Library, Trivandrum
Library Accession No.	5861
Language	Sanskrit
Script	Malayalam

Serial No. 46

Title Proper	Nāṭyaśāstra
Author	Bharata Muni
Institution	University Manuscripts Library, Trivandrum (Travancore University Manuscripts Library)

Library Accession No.	5861
Language	Sanskrit
Script	Sanskrit

Serial No. 47

Title Proper	Nāṭyaśāstra
Author	Bharata Muni
Institution	University Manuscripts Library, Trivandrum (Manuscripts Library, Kariavattam, Trivandrum)
Library Accession No.	5861
Language	Sanskrit
Script	Malayalam

Serial No. 48

Title Proper	Nāṭyaśāstra
Author	Bharata Muni
Institution	University Manuscripts Library, Trivandrum
Library Accession No.	8919
Language	Sanskrit
Script	Malayalam

Serial No. 49

Title Proper	Nāṭyaśāstra
Author	Bharata Muni
Institution	University Manuscripts Library, Trivandrum (Chirukkal Pal. Library)
Library Accession No.	8919
Language	Sanskrit
Script	Malayalam

Serial No. 50

Title Proper	Nāṭyaśāstra

Author	Bharata Muni
Institution	University Manuscripts Library, Trivandrum
Library Accession No.	20412/TPL-1406
Language	Sanskrit
Script	Malayalam

Serial No. 51

Title Proper	Nāṭyaśāstra
Author	Bharata Muni
Institution	University Manuscripts Library, Trivandrum
Library Accession No.	20413/TPL-1407
Language	Sanskrit
Script	Malayalam

Serial No. 52

Title Proper	Nāṭyaśāstra
Author	Bharata Muni
Institution	University Manuscripts Library, Trivandrum
Library Accession No	20414/TPL-1408
Language	Sanskrit
Script	Malayalam

Serial No. 53

Title Proper	Nāṭyaśāstra
Author	Bharata Muni
Institution	University Manuscripts Library, Trivandrum
Library Accession No.	20415/TPL-1409
Language	Sanskrit
Script	Malayalam

Serial No. 54

Title Proper	Nāṭyaśāstra
Author	Bharata Muni
Institution	University Manuscripts Library, Trivandrum
Library Accession No.	20416/TPL-1410
Language	Sanskrit
Script	Malayaḷam

Serial No. 55

Title Proper	Nāṭyaśāstra
Author	Bharata Muni
Institution	University Manuscripts Library, Trivandrum
Library Accession No.	20417/TPL-1411
Language	Sanskrit
Script	Malayalam

Serial No. 56

Title Proper	Nāṭyaśāstra
Author	Bharata Muni
Institution	Durbar Library, Nepal
Library Accession No.	173
Language	Sanskrit
Script	Newari

Serial No. 57

Title Proper	Nāṭyaśāstra with Bharatabhāṣya (Sarasvatihṛdayālaṁkārahāra)
Author	Bharata Muni
Commentator	Nānyadeva
Institution	Bhandarkar Oriental Research Institute, Pune
Library Accession No.	312-111/1869-70

Language Sanskrit
Script Devanagari

Serial No. 58
Title Proper Nāṭyaśāstra
Author Bharata Muni
Institution Bhandarkar Oriental Research Institute, Pune
Library Accession No. 337-69/1873-74
Language Sanskrit
Script Devanagari

Serial No. 59
Title Proper Nāṭyaśāstra
Author Bharata Muni
Institution Bhandarkar Oriental Research Institute, Pune
Library Accession No. 338-39/1916-18
Language Sanskrit
Script Devanagari

Serial No. 60
Title Proper Nāṭyaśāstra
Author Bharata Muni
Institution Bhandarkar Oriental Research Institute, Pune
Library Accession No. 339-36/1916-18
Language Sanskrit
Script Devanagari

Serial No. 61
Title Proper Nāṭyaśāstra
Author Bharata Muni
Institution Bhandarkar Oriental Research Institute, Pune

Library Accession No.	340-37/1916-18
Language	Sanskrit
Script	Kanarese

Serial No: 62

Title Proper	Nāṭyaśāstra
Author	Bharata Muni
Institution	Bhandarkar Oriental Research Institute, Pune
Library Accession No.	341-68/1873-74
Language	Sanskrit
Script	Devanagari

Serial No. 63

Title Proper	Nāṭyaśāstra with Abhinavabhāratī
Author	Bharata Muni
Commentator	Abhinavagupta
Institution	Bhandarkar Oriental Research Institute, Pune
Library Accession No.	342-38/1916-18
Language	Sanskrit
Script	Devanagari

Serial No. 64

Title Proper	Nāṭyaśāstra with Abhinavabhāratī
Author	Bharata Muni
Commentator	Abhinavagupta
Institution	Bhandarkar Oriental Research Institute, Pune
Library Accession No.	343-41/1925-26
Language	Sanskrit
Script	Devanagari

Serial No. 65

Title Proper	Nāṭyaśāstra
Author	Bharata Muni
Institution	Bombay Presidency, Bombay
Library Accession No.	87
Language	Sanskrit

Serial No. 66

Title Proper	Nāṭyaśāstra
Author	Bharata Muni
Institution	Anup Sanskrit Library, Bikaner
Total No. of Pages	F. 7, P. 252
Language	Sanskrit
Script	Devanagari

Serial No. 67

Title Proper	Nāṭyaśāstra
Author	Bharata Muni
Institution	Anup Sanskrit Library, Bikaner
Total No. of Pages	F. 1703
Language	Sanskrit
Script	Devanagari

Serial No. 68

Title Proper	Nāṭyaśāstra
Author	Bharata Muni
Institution	Anup Sanskrit Library, Bikaner
Language	Sanskrit
Script	Devanagari

Serial No. 69

Title Proper	Nāṭyaśāstra
Author	Bharata Muni
Institution	Anup Sanskrit Library, Bikaner

Language	Sanskrit
Script	Devanagari

Serial No. 70

Title Proper	Nāṭyaśāstra (with Telugu meaning)
Author	Bharata Muni
Institution	Adyar Library, Madras
Library Accession No.	24.E.41
Language	Sanskrit
Script	Telugu

Serial No. 71

Title Proper	Nāṭyaśāstra
Author	Bharata Muni
Institution	Adyar Library, Madras
Library Accession No.	34.D.17
Language	Sanskrit
Script	Malayalam

Serial No. 72

Title Proper	Nāṭyaśāstra with Abhinavabhāratī
Author	Bharata Muni
Commentator	Abhinavagupta
Institution	Adyar Library, Madras
Library Accession No.	38.G.14
Language	Sanskrit
Script	Devanagari

Serial No. 73

Title Proper	Nāṭyaśāstra
Author	Bharata Muni
Institution	Adyar Library, Madras
Library Accession No.	39.D.1
Language	Sanskrit
Script	Devanagari

Serial No. 74

Title Proper	Nāṭyaśāstra with Abhinavabhāratī
Author	Bharata Muni
Commentator	Abhinavagupta
Institution	Government Oriental Manuscripts Library, Madras
Library Accession No.	60
Language	Sanskrit

Serial No. 75

Title Proper	Nāṭyaśāstra with Abhinavabhāratī
Author	Bharata Muni
Commentator	Abhinavagupta
Institution	Government Oriental Manuscripts Library, Madras
Library Accession No.	R-2478
Language	Sanskrit
Script	Devanagari

Serial No. 76

Title Proper	Nāṭyaśāstra with Abhinavabhāratī
Author	Bharata Muni
Commentator	Abhinavagupta
Institution	Government Oriental Manuscripts Library, Madras
Library Accession No.	R-2774
Language	Sanskrit
Script	Devanagari

Serial No. 77

Title Proper	Nāṭyaśāstra with Abhinavabhāratī
Author	Bharata Muni
Commentator	Abhinavagupta
Institution	Government Oriental Manuscripts Library, Madras

Library Accession No.	R-2785
Language	Sanskrit
Script	Devanagari

Serial No. 78

Title Proper	Nāṭyaśāstra with Abhinavabhāratī
Author	Bharata Muni
Commentator	Abhinavagupta
Institution	Government Oriental Manuscripts Library, Madras
Library Accession No.	R-2930
Language	Sanskrit
Script	Devanagari

Serial No. 79

Title Proper	Nāṭyaśāstra
Author	Bharata Muni
Institution	Government Oriental Manuscripts Library, Madras
Library Accession No.	R-5271
Language	Sanskrit
Script	Devanagari

Serial No. 80

Title Proper	Nāṭyaśāstra with Nāṭyaśāstravārtika
Author	Bharata Muni
Institution	Government Oriental Manuscripts Library, Madras
Library Accession No.	R-5598
Language	Sanskrit

Serial No. 81

Title Proper	Nāṭyaśāstra
Author	Bharata Muni

Institution	Government Oriental Manuscripts Library, Madras
Library Accession No.	D-12999
Language	Sanskrit
Script	Telugu

Serial No. 82

Title Proper	Nāṭyaśāstra
Author	Bharata Muni
Institution	Government Oriental Manuscripts Library, Madras
Library Accession No.	D-13000
Language	Sanskrit
Script	Telugu

Serial No. 83

Title Proper	Nāṭyaśāstra
Author	Bharata Muni
Institution	Government Oriental Manuscripts Library, Madras
Library Accession No.	D-13001
Language	Sanskrit
Script	Telugu

Serial No. 84

Title Proper	Nāṭyaśāstra
Author	Bharata Muni
Institution	University of Mysore, Oriental Research Institute of Mysore
Library Accession No.	28810/P.472
Language	Sanskrit
Script	Telugu

Serial No. 85

Title Proper	Nāṭyaśāstra
Author	Bharata Muni
Institution	University of Mysore, Oriental Research Institute of Mysore
Library Accession No.	28811/P.2555
Language	Sanskrit
Script	Kanarese

Serial No. 86

Title Proper	Nāṭyaśāstra
Author	Bharata Muni
Institution	University of Mysore, Oriental Research Institute of Mysore
Library Accession No.	28812/P.447212
Language	Sanskrit
Script	Nandi Nagari

Serial No. 87

Title Proper	Nāṭyaśāstra
Author	Bharata Muni
Institution	University of Mysore, Oriental Research Institute of Mysore
Library Accession No.	28813/P.5741/3A
Language	Sanskrit
Script	Telugu

Serial No. 88

Title Proper	Nāṭyaśāstra
Author	Bharata Muni
Institution	University of Mysore, Oriental Research Institute of Mysore
Library Accession No.	E28814/B.1062/1

Language	Sanskrit
Script	Kanarese

Serial No. 89

Title Proper	Nāṭyaśāstra with Abhinavabhāratī
Author	Bharata Muni
Commentator	Abhinavagupta
Institution	University of Mysore, Oriental Research Institute of Mysore
Library Accession No.	28815/P.5741/3B
Language	Sanskrit
Script	Telugu

Serial No. 90

Title Proper	Nāṭyaśāstra with Abhinavabhāratī
Author	Bharata Muni
Commentator	Abhinavagupta
Institution	University of Mysore, Oriental Research Institute of Mysore
Library Accession No.	2816/B.1062/2
Language	Sanskrit
Script	Kanarese

Serial No. 91

Title Proper	Nāṭyaśāstra
Author	Bharata Muni
Institution	Akhil Bharatiya Sanskrit Parishad, Lucknow
Library Accession No.	863
Language	Sanskrit
Script	Devanagari

Serial No. 92

Title Proper	Nāṭyaśāstra
Author	Bharata Muni

Institution	India Office Library, London
Library Accession No.	5200 (1443 a)
Language	Sanskrit
Script	Devanagari

Serial No. 93

Title Proper	Nāṭyaśāstra
Author	Bharata Muni
Institution	Punjab University Library, Lahore
Library Accession No.	3147
Language	Sanskrit
Script	Tamil

Serial No. 94

Title Proper	Nāṭyaśāstra with Abhinavabhāratī
Author	Bharata Muni
Commentator	Abhinavagupta
Institution	Sampurnananda Sanskrit University Library (Sarasvati Bhavan), Varanasi
Library Accession No.	40765
Language	Sanskrit
Script	Devanagari

Serial No. 95

Title Proper	Nāṭyavedavivṛtti
Commentator	Abhinavagupta
Institution	Sampurnananda Sanskrit University Library (Sarasvati Bhavan), Varanasi
Library Accession No.	40766
Language	Sanskrit
Script	Devanagari

Serial No. 96

Title Proper	Abhinavabhāratī
Commentator	Abhinavagupta

Institution	Sampurnananda Sanskrit University Library (Sarasvati Bhavan), Varanasi
Library Accession No.	40767
Language	Sanskrit
Script	Devanagari

Serial No. 97

Title Proper	Abhinavabhāratī
Commentator	Abhinavagupta
Institution	Sampurnananda Sanskrit University Library (Sarasvati Bhavan), Varanasi
Library Accession No.	40768
Language	Sanskrit
Script	Devanagari

Serial No. 98

Title Proper	Nāṭyaśāstra
Author	Bharata Muni
Institution	Sampurnananda Sanskrit University Library (Sarasvati Bhavan), Varanasi
Library Accession No.	42727
Language	Sanskrit
Script	Devanagari

Serial No. 99

Title Proper	Nāṭyaśāstra with Abhinavabhāratī
Author	Bharata Muni
Commentator	Abhinavagupta
Institution	Andhra University Library, Waltair
Library Accession No.	PPS-249
Language	Sanskrit
Script	Tamil

Serial No. 100

Title Proper	Nāṭyaśāstra
Author	Bharata Muni
Institution	Vrindavan Research Institute, Vrindavan
Library Accession No.	1140
Language	Sanskrit
Script	Devanagari

Serial No. 101

Title Proper	Nāṭyaśāstra
Author	Bharata Muni
Institution	American Oriental Society, New Haven (U.S.A.)
Library Accession No.	2431 (H-2284)
Language	Sanskrit
Script	Devanagari

Serial No. 102

Title Proper	Nāṭyaśāstra
Author	Bharata Muni
Institution	Harvard University Library, Harvard
Library Accession No.	2284
Language	Sanskrit
Script	Devanagari

Serial No. 103

Title Proper	Nāṭyaśāstra
Author	Bharata Muni
Institution	Vishveshvarananda Vedic Research Institute, Hoshiarpur
Library Accession No.	6280
Language	Sanskrit
Script	Malayalam

Serial No. 104

Title Proper	Nāṭyaśāstra
Author	Bharata Muni
Institution	National Archives, Kathmandoo
Mss. No.	P1592
Language	Sanskrit
Script	Newari

Serial No. 105

Title Proper	Nāṭyaśāstra
Author	Bharata Muni
Institution	National Archives, Kathmandoo
Mss. No.	RL No. A 19/2
Language	Sanskrit
Script	Newari

Serial No. 106

Title Proper	Nāṭyaśāstra
Author	Bharata Muni
Institution	National Archives, Kathmandoo
Mss. No.	173
Language	Sanskrit
Script	Newari

Serial No. 107

Title Proper	Nāṭyaśāstra
Author	Bharata Muni
Institution	National Archives, Kathmandoo
Mss. No.	R.L.-A-1911
Language	Sanskrit
Script	Newari

Serial No. 108

Title Proper	Nāṭyaśāstra
Author	Bharata Muni

Institution	National Archives, Kathmandoo
Mss. No.	5-996
Language	Sanskrit
Script	Newari

Serial No. 109

Title Proper	Nāṭyaśāstra
Author	Bharata Muni
Institution	National Archives, Kathmandoo
Mss. No.	Pam 1140
Language	Sanskrit
Script	Devanagari

Serial No. 110

Title Proper	Nāṭyaśāstra
Author	Bharata Muni
Institution	National Archives, Kathmandoo
Mss. No.	CA-316 vi 6
Language	Sanskrit
Script	Newari

Serial No. 111

Title Proper	Nāṭyaśāstra
Author	Bharata Muni
Institution	National Archives, Kathmandoo
Mss. No.	5-998
Language	Sanskrit
Script	Newari

Serial No. 112

Title Proper	Nāṭyaśāstra
Author	Bharata Muni
Institution	National Archives, Kathmandoo
Mss. No.	3-97
Language	Sanskrit
Script	Newari

INDEX

abhaṅga 125, 126
ābharaṇakṛt 95
ābhāsa 151
abhidhā 133
Abhilaṣatārthacintāmaṇi 119
Abhinavabhāratī 28, 29, 34, 35, 37, 114, 129, 132, 133, 138, 141, 149, 154, 156, 157
Abhinavagupta 28, 29, 35, 36, 78, 114, 115, 122, 131, 133, 137, 138, 145, 148, 149, 151, 152, 154, 155, 156, 157, 158, 159
abhinaya 74, 80, 82, 89, 93, 99, 122, 69
Abhinayacandrikā 124
Abhinayadarpaṇa 122
ābhyantara 81, 86
adbhuta 90
ādhibhautika 48, 57
ādhidaivika 48, 57
Adil Shāh 120
adhyātma 88, 89
ādhyātmika 48, 57
āgamas 17
āgamic text 16
Agastya 95
agni (fire) 19, 49
Agni Purāṇa 116, 126, 127
Agrawala, V.S. 114
āhārya 55, 69, 99
Ahobala 120
Ain-e-Akbarī 120
Ajanta 109
ākāśa 12, 50
ākāśikā 67
Alaknanda 162
alaṁkāra 71, 72, 85, 131, 167
alaṁkāraśāstra 131
ālambana 153
alasākanyās 126
alātacakra 105
alaukika 151, 156
alaukikajñāna 143
Amaravati 108
Amṛtamanthana samavakāra 62
analysis of the body 65-66
ānanda 14, 147, 151, 152, 153, 155
ānanda tāṇḍava iconography 14
Ānandavardhana 131, 133, 145, 148, 149, 156, 167
anatomy, analysis of 65-66
āṇavamala 153
aṇḍa 51
aṅga 10, 66, 80, 122, 125
aṅgahāras 7, 14, 63, 68
āṅgika (body) 55, 68, 69, 73, 82, 92, 99, 122
āṅgikābhinaya 7, 18, 67, 79, 121
Aṅgiras 95
anibaddha 123
aṅkiya nāṭas 131
aṅkura 85
Annales de Musé Guimet 32
antaḥ-salilā 58
antarātman 22
anti-heroes 94
anubhāva 87, 138, 153, 154

anucarita 103
anucaritam 80
anudātta 72
anukaraṇa 88, 138, 140, 166
anukathana 103, 138
anukīrtana 96, 103, 138, 166
anukṛṣṭi 103
anupāya 153
anusandhāna 139
anusmaraṇa 48
anuvyavasāya 166
aparā 156
Aparājitapṛcchā 125
apsaras 107, 108
ārabhaṭī 81
āraṁbha 76
Ardhanārīśvara 107, 150
Aristotelian unities 69
Aristotle 133
Art Experience 144
artha 21, 41, 57
artha-kāma 84
arthaprakṛti 75, 76, 77, 80
Arthaśāstra 114
arūpa 22
āsanas 67
Asiatic Society 35
āśramas 21
Aṣṭādhyāyī 114
āsvāda 103, 161
Aśvaghoṣa 17
Atharvaveda 14, 52
ātman 51, 52, 104, 165
Ātreya 95
avamarśa 78
Avantivarman 137
avasthā 75, 76, 130
avyakta 21, 54, 55, 165
Āyurveda 19, 24, 119
Āyurvedic system 19

Bādarāyaṇa 114
baddha 123
bāhya 85, 86
ballad singers 9
bandha 80
bandha nṛtya 80
Belur 108
Bhagavatamelas 131
Bhāgīrathī 162
Bhaktirasāmṛtasindhu
Bhāmaha 131, 158, 167
bhaṅgas 125
Bharadvāja 95
Bharata, question of authorship 1-12, 162; text attributed 5; world view 26, 55-56 system of exercise 67, see also under *Nāṭyaśāstra*
Bharatabhāṣya 119
bhāratī 81
Bharhut 106
Bhāsa 102, 137
Bhaṭṭa Indurāja 149
Bhaṭṭa Lollaṭa 138, 139-141, 143, 147
Bhaṭṭa Nāyaka 138, 145, 146, 147, 148, 152, 154
Bhaṭṭa Tauta 138, 149
Bhaṭṭa Udbhaṭa 131
bhāndas 131
bhaumī 67
bhāva 25, 50, 81, 84, 85, 87, 98, 160
bhāvanā 146, 148
Bhoja 78, 116, 129, 158, 159
bhojakatva 146
bhramarīs 122
bhṛṅgāra 15, 63
bhujaṅgatrāsita 14
bhūtas 19, 61
Bibliotheca Indica series 32
bīja 49, 50, 51, 52, 53, 73, 74, 75, 77, 104, 105, 125, 128, 165
bindu 53, 73, 74, 75, 77, 105, 125, 126
Blake 26
Bodhi tree 107
Bradley 133
Brahmā 95, 107
Brahmā's *samādhi* 95
brahmamaṇḍala 14, 17, 124

Brahman 8, 11, 15, 51, 52, 53, 54, 61, 145, 146, 149
Brāhmaṇas 10, 16, 165
brahmāṇḍa 51
Brāhmanical ritual (*yajña*) 113, 124
brahmasthāna 14, 60
brahmasūtra 14
Bṛhaddeśī 118
Bṛhadīśvara 127
Buddha 24, 106, 107
Butcher 133

camatkāra 151, 152
camatkāra parambhoga 152
Caṇḍālas 18
Caṇḍikā 15
Caraka 119
cārī 67
cārīs 68
Carnatic music 102, 121
carvaṇā 152
cetana 51, 84
chandovidhāna 70
chandovit 91
Chidambaram temple 34
citra 125, 126
citrabandha 80
citrābhinaya 82, 86, 87, 98, 130
citrakāra 95
citrasūtras 127
citravit 91
Classical Sanskrit 18
Coomaraswamy 2

dādra 121
Daityas 61
daivika 69, 90, 96, 117
Dāmodara 123
Daṇḍin 131, 158, 167
darśana 139
Daśarūpaka 32, 74, 129, 159
daśarūpalakṣaṇaṁ 73
daśāvatāra 121
daśāvatāra hastas 121
Dattila 8, 114, 115, 118
see also Dhūrtila
Dattilam 114, 117, 131
De, S.K. 6, 114
deśī 118
deśīkaraṇa 119, 122
Dhanañjaya 129, 158, 159
dharma 21, 41, 57
dharma kāma 84
dharmīs 81, 94
dhrupad 121
dhruva songs 86, 92, 93
Dhūrtila 11, 114, 115, 117
dhvaja 15
dhvani 132, 145, 148, 167
Dhvanyāloka 132, 133, 148, 149, 156, 157
ḍima 129
dīpaka 71
divine consciousness 156
drama, purpose of 148
Drāviḍa 124
dṛṣṭi 66
Durgā 108
dvibhaṅga 125

Eckhart, Meister 26
ethno-linguistic data 18
fifth Veda 10

Gaekwad Oriental series 36
gāna 92
gandha 84
gandharva 91, 107, 108
gāndharva 92, 117, 126, 131
Gaṇeśa 15
Gaṇeśvara 15
Gaṅgā 5, 162
gaṇita 24
garbha 53, 75, 78, 125, 165

gati 68
Gauḍīya Vaiṣṇavism 159
geya 92
ghana 76
gharānās 121
Ghosh, M.M. 6, 33, 35, 114
ghungroos 123
Gilgit manuscripts 31, 36
Gīta Govinda 128, 159
Gnoli, R. 36, 133
Goethe 32
gopurams 34
grāma 92, 120
grāma rāgas 118
Grosset, J. 33
guha 97, 165
Guhyakas 61
Guṇacandra 130
guṇas 19, 20, 71
Gupta 107

Hāla 137
Halebid 108
Hall 32
hallisaka 129
Hampi 108
Harihara 107
hariṇapluta 70
Harivaṁśa 129
Harṣa 137
hastas 66
Hastalakṣaṇadīpikā 124
Hastamuktāvali 124
haṭhayoga 67
hāva 85
Haymann 32
helā 85
heroines 94
heroes 94
Hillebrandt 114
Hindustani music 102, 121
Hiriyana 144
Hṛdayadarpaṇa 145, 147
Hṛdayaviśrānti 155, 156

icchopāya 153
Indra 15, 61
Indra's banner festival 9
instrumental music 92
Islamic Calligraphy 109, 110
Islamic geometrical designs 109
Īśvara Pratyabhijñā kārikā 140, 145
Īśvara Pratyabhijñā Vimarśinī 149
īṣvastravit 91
itihāsa 3
itivṛtta 50, 73, 78, 79, 80, 98, 104
jaḍa 51
Jagannātha 131, 158, 159
Jaina Tīrthaṅkaras 24
jakkadi 123
jala 19
Jamadagni 95
japa 16, 96
jarjara 61, 63
jātis 92
Jayadeva 159
Jayāpīḍa 137
Jayasenāpati 122
jīva (life) 51
Jīva Gosvāmin 159
Jones, William 32
Junagarh rock inscriptions 24
jyotiṣa 24

kaiśikī 81
kakṣāvibhāga 68, 69, 72, 73, 75, 99, 127, 128
kalā 25
kāla 153 154
Kālidāsa 2, 102, 110, 137
kalpanā 40
kalpavṛkṣa 129
kāma 21, 41, 57, 84, 85,
kāmatantra 86

kampita 72
Kane, P.V. 114
kaṇṭha 72
Kaṇva 95
kapha 19, 84
karaṇas 7, 34, 62, 63, 68, 70, 121, 122, 123, 125, 126, 127,
karmamala 153
Kārtikeya 15
kāru (carpenter) 95
karuṇa 107
Kashi Sanskrit series 35
Kashmiri commentators 160
Kashmiri Śaivism 35, 132, 139, 149, 150, 151
Kaṭhopaniṣad 22, 55
kavi 95
kavitā 40
kāvya 163, 167
Kāvyamālā edition 33
Keith, A.B. 6, 114
Kenopaniṣad 54
khayāl 121
kinnaras 126
kirātas 18
Kitab-e-Nau Rasa 120
Kodaṇḍa Rāma 126
Kohala 8, 11, 114, 122
Konarka 108
Konow, Stein 6, 114
Kosala 18
Kośī 18
kriyopāya 153
kṛśāśva 114
Kṛṣṇa 15
kṛti 121
Kubera 15
Kuiper, F.B.J. 6, 15
Kulaśekhara 37
Kumbha 120
Kuntaka 131, 159
Kuṣāṇa 107
kuśīlava 95
kutapa 68
kuṭilaka 15
kūṭiyāṭṭam 37
kūttambalams 124

lakṣaṇa 70, 131, 133
Lakṣmaṇagupta 149
lāsya 121
Lath, Mukund 117
Levi, Sylvan 33, 34, 114
līlas 131
liṅgam 108
liṅgas 107
Locana 132, 133
loka 72, 88, 89
lokadharma 89
lokadharmī 69, 71, 81,
loka-vyavahāra 88, 90
Longinus 26

Macdonnel 6
māch 131
Mahābhārata 18, 39, 114
Mahābhāṣya 114
Maheśa 107, 114
Maheśvara 8, 14, 149, 152
Mahimabhaṭṭa 131
mālyakṛt 95
manas 55, 84, 125
mānasollāsa 120, 125
Mandākini 162
maṇḍalas 67
maṅgala 96
manopāya 153
mantra mūrtis 111
mantras 153
Manu 95
mānuṣī 69, 90, 96, 117
mārga 118, 119
Mārkaṇḍeya 95
Mataṅga 118, 120
mati 15
Mātṛgupta 130

māyīyamala 153
mayūralalita 70
Mayūrānanda rasa nyāya 151
Medhā 15
micro-intervals 92
Mīmāṁsā 132, 139
Mohammed Raza 120
Mohammed Shah 120
mokṣa 21, 41, 57, 106, 160
mokṣa kāma 84
Monier-Williams 42
muhūrtas 79
mukha 75, 78
mukuṭa-kāraka 95
mūrcchanā 92, 118, 120

nābhi 53
nāch 131
nāda-Brahman 111
nāḍikās 79
Nāgamalī-i-Ashrafī 120
Nāgara 124
nakṣatras 121
nāma 57
Nandikeśvara 121, 122, 123
Nānyadeva 119
nārīkuñja bandha 80
nartaka 91
Nartana Nirṇaya 123
naṭa 95
Nāṭakalakṣaṇaratnakośa 129, 130, 131, 159
nāṭakīya 95
naṭamaṇḍapa 124
naṭanam 121
Naṭarāja 14, 108, 126
naṭiyita 86
nāṭya 14, 25, 40, 44, 69, 81, 121, 166
Nāṭyadarpaṇa 129, 130, 131, 159
nāṭyadharmi 69
nāṭyakāra 95
nāṭyamaṇḍapa 16
Nāṭyaśāstra, authentic text 35; discovery of manuscript 31-37; search 35; sources of 13-26; pretext and context 13-26; primary text 28-46; implicit and explicit text 47-100; text and interpreters 137-161; text and creativity 102-112; text 113-134, 162
—, location of manuscript 37
—, a work of single author 6
—, *paramparā* of 162, 163
Nāṭyatattva 89
Nāṭyaveda 8, 88, 89
nāṭyavidhāna 88
nautaṅkis 85
nāyaka 85
nāyikā 85
Nepal 31, 164
nibaddha 123
nirṛti 15
nirvahaṇa 78
nirvāṇa 106
nirvikalpa 150
nivṛtyaṅkura 86
niyama 93
niyataphalaprāpti 71
niyati 15
nṛtta 67, 121, 123, 167
Nṛttaratnāvali 122

pada 117
Pahlava 18
Pāla 107
palais 120
Palampet 127
Paṇḍarīka Viṭṭhala 123
Pāṇḍey, K.C. 6
Pāṇini 18, 114
pāns 120
parā 156
Parab, Kashinath Panduranga 33
Parambanan temple 127
paramparā 30, 116, 162, 163
parāparā 156
parārūpa 22, 57, 112

parāvāk 156
paripālavas 9
parokṣa 85, 86
Pārśvadeva 120, 122
Pārvatī 15, 107
patākā 77
Patañjali 20, 114
pāṭhya 13, 70
pereni nṛtya 122
phalāgama 77
phalayoga 77
physical space 61, 62
piṇḍibandha 63, 80
piśācas 61
Pitāmaha 8
pitta 19, 84
pradarśana 87
prahasana 129
Prajāpati 51, 157
Prajñānananda, Swami 94
prakarī 77
prakāśa 152
Prakrit 18
Prākrit poetry 13
prakṛti 144
pramāṇa 142
pramātṛ 142
prameya 142
prāṇa pratiṣṭhā 17
prāptisambhava 76
pratimā-lakṣaṇa 127
pratimukha 75, 78
pratyakṣa 85, 86
pratyaṅga 122
pravṛttis 18, 68, 69, 71, 81, 94
prayāga 113, 162
prāyaścitta 97
prayatna 76
prayoga 40, 89, 95, 117, 168
prayoga śāstra 42
prayoktṛ 89
prekṣaka 91
pṛthvī 19
pūjā 8, 16, 17, 62, 113
purāṇa 3
Purāṇas 24, 41, 116, 126, 137, 167
Purūravas 15, 97, 113
puruṣa 51, 52, 53, 73, 74, 78, 105, 125, 144
puruṣārthas 21, 41, 48
Puruṣasūkta 51, 52
pūrvābhāsa yojanā 140
pūrvaraṅga 63, 64, 75, 93, 96, 130
pūrvāvṛta carita 88

rāga 120, 153
rāga-rāgiṇi 120
Raghavan, V. 82
rajaka 95
rājan 91
rajas 153
Rājaśekhara 158
rājasevaka 91
Rāma 147, 148
Rāmacandra 129, 130, 158
Ramakrishna Kavi, M. 6, 34, 36, 133
Ramaswami Sastri 34, 36
Rāmāyaṇa 18, 114, 128
rasa 9, 19, 25, 50, 64, 65, 71, 72, 74, 84, 98, 138, 139, 141, 153, 155, 160,
rāsa dance 15, 131
rāsaka 129
rasaniṣpatti 138
Rāvaṇa 147, 148
Regnaud, P. 32, 33
Ṛgveda 13, 49, 51
Ṛgvedic formulation 22
Ṛgvedic myth 15
Rhetoric Sanscrite 33
Risāla-i-Rāgadarpaṇa 120
Rudradāman 24
rūpa 57, 75, 84
Rūpa Gosvāmin 159
rūpaka 71
rūpa pratirūpa 22

śabda 13, 84
śabdavit 91

sabhāstava 23
sādhaka 91
sādhana 57, 91
sādhāraṇīkaraṇa 133, 146, 149, 152, 154,
Sāgaranandin 78, 129, 130, 158
sāhitya 40, 166, 167
sahṛdaya 161
Sahṛdayadarpaṇa 147
Sahṛdayāloka 132, 133, 148,
Śaiva metaphysics 144
Śaiva monism 145
Śaiva philosophy 140, 151, 153
Śaiva Siddhānta 160
Śaivite temples 137
Śaka 18
śākhā 85
śakti 151, 156
Śakuntalā 106
śālā 57, 60
śālabhañjikā 126
Śālikarṇa 8, 114
sama 67
sama-bhaṅga 126
samādhi 22, 59
samālocana 40
sāmānya 83
sāmānyābhinaya 82, 83, 86, 87, 98, 130
Samarāṅgasūtradhāra 125
Sāmaveda 14
samavedana 161
Sāṁkhya 132, 139, 144
sampradāyas 121
sañcāri bhāva 138, 154
Sanchi 106, 108
sandhi 75, 76, 78, 80
Śāṇḍilya 11
saṅgīta 45, 72, 166, 167
Saṅgītadarpaṇa 123
Saṅgītakaumudī 120
Saṅgīta Mallikā 120
Saṅgītanārāyaṇa 120
Saṅgītapārijāta 120
Saṅgīta Rāja 120
Saṅgītaratnākara 115, 119, 120
Saṅgīta samayasāra 120
saṅkalpa 120
Sanskrit drama 37
śānta 125
śānta rasa 35, 98, 155
Sarasvatī 15, 16, 61
śarīra 52, 78, 80, 96, 104, 165
Śārṅgadeva 118, 122, 123
Śārṅgapāṇi 127
śāstra 39-43, 163
śāstra of *prayoga* 38, 95
Śāstrīya nṛtya 40, 43
śāstrīya saṅgīta 43
Śātakarṇi 114
Śatapathabrāhmaṇa 15
saṭṭaka 129
sattva 147, 153
sattvam 55
sāttvika 14, 55, 69, 82, 83, 98, 99
sāttvikābhinaya 83
sātvatī 81
sauṣṭhava 67
senāpati 23
śeṣa 61
Shakespeare 133
Sharma, Premlata 94, 119
Shivadatta, Pandit 33
siddham 88
Siddhārtha 106
siddhi 15, 90
Śilālin 114
Śilappadikāram 120
śilpa 25, 125, 166, 167, 126
Śilpaprakāśa 125
Śilpasāriṇī 125
Śilpaśāstra 44, 125, 126, 127
śiras 72
Sittanavasal 109
Śiva 14, 15, 61, 107, 114, 126
—, cosmic poet 148
Śiva-Sadāśiva 152
smṛti 15
smṛtis 39
Someśvara 119, 122
sparśa 84

Śrīśaṅkuka 138, 141, 142, 143, 146, 147, 141-144
śṛṅgāra 108
Śṛṅgāra Prakāśa 116, 129, 159
śruti 39, 92, 120, 163
śrutis 29
stage, division of 127
sthāna 67, 72, 125
sthāyi bhāva 8, 59, 60, 64, 65, 72, 74, 81, 83, 138, 139, 140, 142, 143, 152, 153, 159
stūpa 62, 105, 106, 111
Sudhākalaśa 120
Śūdraka 137
śūdras 10, 96
sukumāra 69, 121
śūnya 106
surasundarīs 126
Sūrya 15, 49
Śuśruta 119
sūtradhāra 95, 96, 97
sūtras 30, 125
svabhāva 150
svabhāvas tajyate 80
svāmin 23
svātantrayavāda
svara 73, 92, 117, 120
svarita 72

Taittirīya Āraṇyaka 52
Taittirīya Upaniṣad 151
tāla 92, 117, 120
tamas 153
tāṇḍava 69, 93, 121
Tāṇḍavalakṣaṇam 7, 34
Taṇḍu 8
Tantras 49
Tantrasamuccaya 125
tanu 70
tapas 57, 97
ṭappā 121
taṭastha 59
textual tradition in India 38, 116
Theatre hall, construction of 124
Theatre indien 33
Theatre of the Hindus 32
thumri 121
Tibet 31, 164
tillānā 121
time 3, 98
Tiruvanmalai 127
Treate du Bharata sur la theatre text Sanscrit edition critique 33
Triangle 14
Tribhaṅga 125, 126
trikāla 21, 79
triloka 21, 60, 79, 128
Trimūrti 107, 108
Tripathy, K.D. 36
Trivandrum Collection 36
Types of characters 94

udātta 72
Udbhaṭa 36, 133
uddīpana 153
Ujjain 35
Ujjvalanīlamaṇi 159
ultimate reality 150
upamā 71
upāṅgas 10, 66, 80, 122, 125
Upaniṣadic world-view 57
Upaniṣads 21, 24, 54, 55, 83, 113, 165
uparūpakas 129
uras 72
Urvaśī 15, 97, 113
Utpalācārya 140, 149, 151
Utpaladeva 144
utplavanas 122

vācika 55, 69, 92, 98, 99
Vaiṣṇava āgamas 160
Vaiṣṇavakaraṇa 14
Vaiṣṇavasthāna 14
vāk 61
Vālmīki 2, 95, 110
Vāmana 131, 167
varṇa 92

vārtā 88
Varuṇa 15, 16
Vasiṣṭha 95
Vāsiṣṭhīputra Puḷmāvi 24
vāstu 166
vāstupuruṣa maṇḍala 124
Vāstuśāstra 44, 45
vāta 19, 84
Vatsya 11
vāyu 16, 19
Vedānta 132, 139, 144
Vedāntic conception 149
Vedantic school 145
Vedas 10, 11, 13, 24, 26, 29, 113
Vedic dialogues 113
Vedic intonation 30
Vedic knowledge 11
Vedic *mantras* 96
Vedic rituals 67
Vedic Sanskrit 18
Vedic texts 4, 8
Vedic *yajña* 14, 16, 20
vedikā 16
vedis 60
verbal texts 4
veṣakāra 95
veśara 124
veśyā 91
vibhāva 87, 138, 153, 154
vidhāna 91, 93
vidhi 91, 93
vidūṣaka 15, 95
vimarśa 78
viniyoga 67, 78
vismaya 106
Viṣṇu 14, 15, 61, 107, 126
ViṣṇudharmottaraPurāṇa 126, 127, 167
Viṣṇu images 108
viśrānti 154
Viśvāmitra 95
Viśvanātha 131, 158, 159
vocal music 92
Vṛttalakṣaṇa 70
vṛścika 126
vṛttis 68, 68, 71, 81, 94
vybhicāri bhāva 9, 64, 81, 108, 128, 138, 142, 154, 159
vyakta 22, 165
vyāla 126
Vyāsa 2
vyañjana 65
vyāyāma 67, 122

Weber 114
Wilson 32, 34

yajña 8, 49, 51, 57, 60, 62, 78, 124, 165
yajñavit 91
Yajurveda 14
Yakṣagāna 131
Yakṣas 61
Yakṣīs 107
yamaka 71
Yavana 18
Yeats 26
yoga 56, 132, 139, 165
Yogasūtra 20
yogīs 107
yojana 139, 140
yuvarāja 23